D0892099

Office and Corporate Interiors

Edition 2005

Author: Pilar Chueca
Publisher: Carles Broto
Editorial Coordinator: Jacobo Krauel
Graphic designer & production: Dimitris Kottas
Text: contributed by the architects, edited by Amber Ockrassa and
Jacobo Krauel

© Carles Broto i Comerma
Jonqueres, 10, 1-5
08003 Barcelona, Spain
Tel.: +34 93 301 21 99
Fax: +34-93-301 00 21
E-mail: info@linksbooks.net
www. linksbooks.net

Office and Corporate Interiors

Index

Introduction

The work environment, as a space for professional and interpersonal exchange, has undergone dramatic changes in recent years. The continuing swift pace of developments in communication technology, with a new, more timeless, ubiquitous and portable handling of information, has greatly contributed to these changes. Gone are the bulky file cabinets and expansive tables of yesteryear, with work surfaces having been reduced to the size of a computer. Tele-work and videoconferencing are further indications of this omnipresence.

These, and a host of additional concerns particular to office design, greet the architect and interior designers when drawing up the plans for a new workspace. The company's corporate identity, for example, must be somehow translated into the volumes of the interior spaces, as well as of the building as a whole. The modern office also requires versatility and dynamism – it must be flexible enough to quickly adapt to a range of uses. It must be aesthetically pleasing, and should encourage interpersonal communication amongst employees, while significantly lessening outdated hierarchical barriers.

In short, this is a concise, yet wide-ranging, volume, bringing together examples of renovated spaces as well as entirely new ground plans – proposals which comprise an invaluable source of inspiration and a concentrated study of the challenges involved in creating new workspaces.

THAM VIDEGÅRD HANSSON

IN COLLABORATION WITH SNOWCRASH

Snowcrash Office and showroom

PHOTOGRAPHS: ÅKE E: SON LINDMAN   **Stockholm, Sweden**

Tham Videgård Hansson Architects were commissioned to remodel an old industrial building in Stockholm for Snowcrash, a Swedish-Finnish company that develops concepts and products for work and home.

The building offered a full 28x42x3 m pillar deck floor with light from the east, west and south. Apart from the open office and showroom, the brief also included a workshop, a prototype atelier, and an apartment for visiting designers.

The new office layout combines an effective open office with defined rooms of varying size. The aim was to create an optimum work environment, and aspects such as acoustics, lighting and air were studied.

The main design element is a continuous, free formed, glass wall inserted into the existing warehouse structure. The undulating glass core creates defined places within the premises: showroom, east office, kitchen, west office. Simultaneously it constitutes a link in between all areas, both visually and logistically.

Since no doors have been placed in the glass facing the open office, the amount of accessible free wall surface is increased and the risk of disturbance between the meeting room and the office is minimized. As a result, a visual and spatial pause is created (as a buffer) in the transition from work to meeting. Deep grey in the passageways underlines this spatial contrast. The color scheme is otherwise atelier-like; with light, neutral tones.

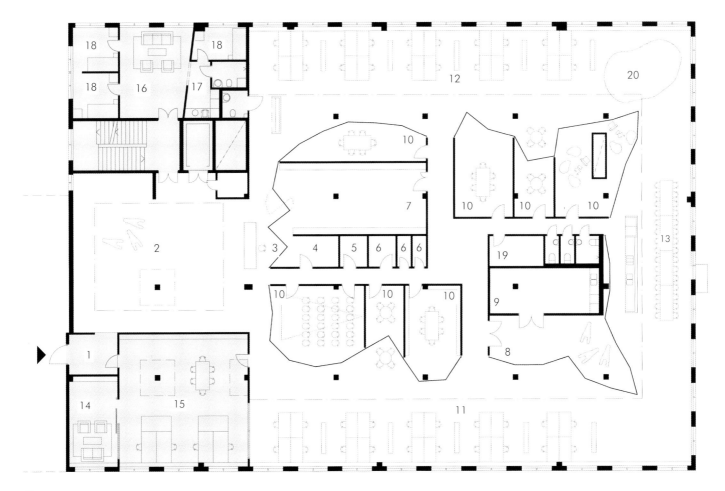

Plan

1. Entrance
2. Showroom
3. Reception
4. Copy room
5. Furniture storage
6. Phone booth
7. Storage
8. Prototype atelier
9. Workshop
10. Project & meeting room
11. Office - Design development
12. Office - Administration
13. Canteen
14. Meeting room
15. Office & art meeting room
16. Sitting room
17. Pantry
18. Guestroom
19. Computer room
20. Cloud

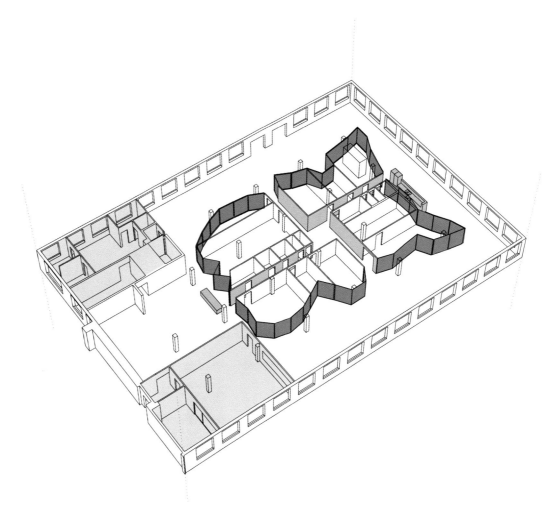

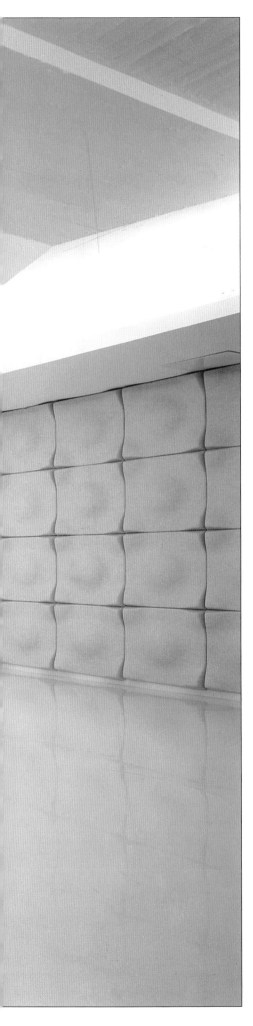

With the initial idea of creating a contemporary environment that communicates the Snowcrash state of mind, the architects opted for open and fluid solutions rather than a closed and final form. Designed as one continuous space, the architecture enhances the impression of a company where everyone works together, 'interweaving' professional skills.

The staff canteen and the entrance, pictured opposite, are floored in glossy epoxy. Both the kitchen counter in the canteen and the reception desk in the entrance are covered in green athletic rubber flooring. Sculptural Chip lounges by Teppo Asikainen and Ilkka Terho grace the reception area.

The walls of the War Room, with the irregular glass partitions, are clad in blackboard for mapping out strategies and ideas.

MITCHELL & GIURGOLA

Lighthouse National Headquarters

PHOTOGRAPHS: JEFF GOLDBERG/ESTO PHOTOGRAPHICS

New York, USA

The design of the new building for the headquarters of the Lighthouse company —the world leader in the organization of visual rehabilitation programs— is equally sensitive to the aesthetics and to the special needs of the users of the center. The building includes an ophthalmology center, a center for child and pre-school development, a technological center for the occupational training, classrooms, offices, an applied research institute, a teaching and conference center (with an auditorium/theater with capacity for 237 people), a music school and a library.

This building is a national model of accessibility that easily exceeds the requirements of the Americans with Disabilities Act (ADA). Each detail was designed with special attention to the diversity of the users of the center. Both on the exterior and in the interior the building brings together the accessibility needs of those who suffer visual, auditory and motor impairments.

The interior includes the use of contrasting colors and textures on the floor, and special materials to mark the steps of the staircase, changes of corridor, openings in the walls, direction, level and intersections. This special attention toward the patients and users is complemented with maps and tactile signs, and an auditorium equipped with an intensified descriptive audio system.

The upper part of the building is covered in bricks with elegant stone borders framing the windows. Like a lighthouse, the windows articulate the south-east corner of the building, and their orientation toward Lexington Avenue reinforces the presence of the center. In the design of this center the architects sought a formula that made it possible to introduce as much natural lighting as possible in the interior staircases, the corridors and the shared office spaces. Finally, it was decided to conserve a part of the existing steel structure that has now been expanded in the design of the new building.

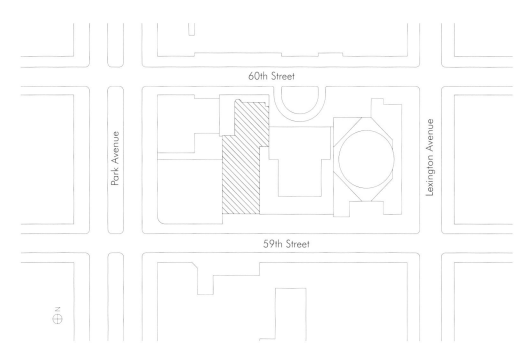

This fifteen-story building was designed to incorporate interior and exterior elements to help people with visual disabilities or limited mobility. The photograph below shows the building before its renovation.

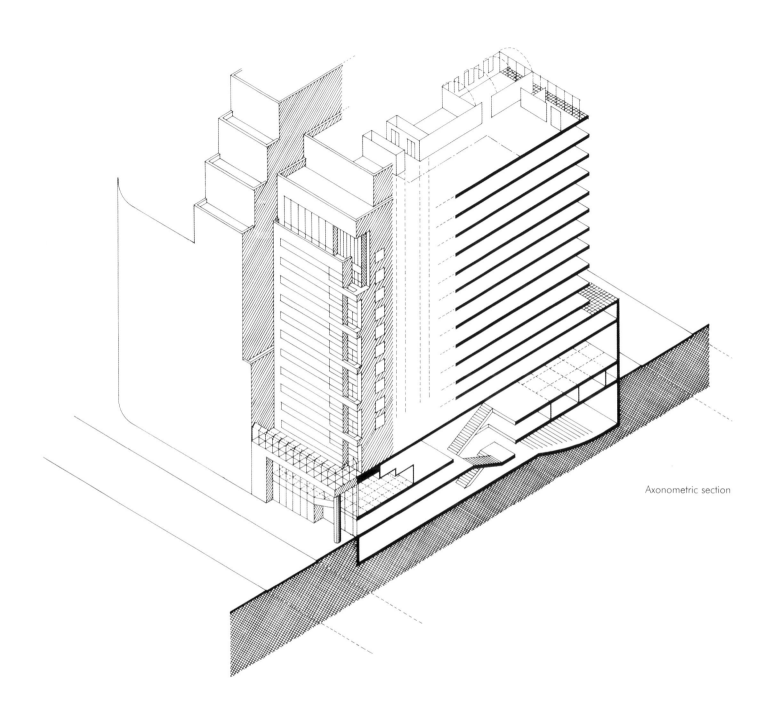

Axonometric section

Mezzanine level plan
1. Cafe
2. Multi-Purpose
3. Kitchen
4. WC

Auditorium level plan
1. Auditorium
2. Dreesing room
3. Projection room
4. Mechanical

11th floor plan
1. Offices
2. Open office
3. Reception
4. Mechanical
5. Conference room
6. Vision Lab
7. Class room

Mezzanine level plan

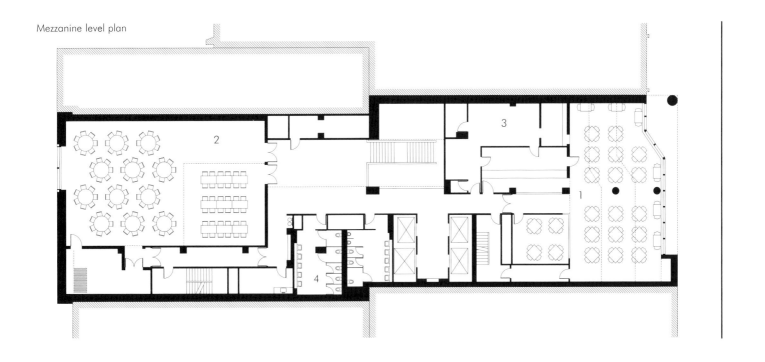

Auditorium level plan

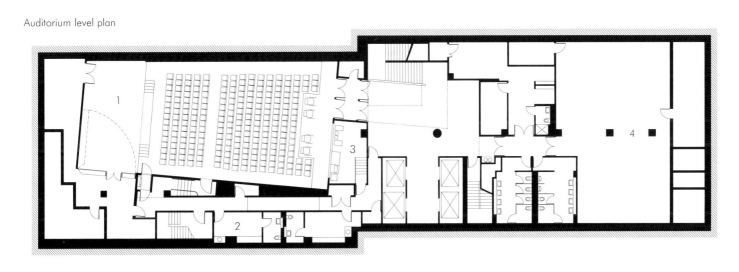

11th floor plan

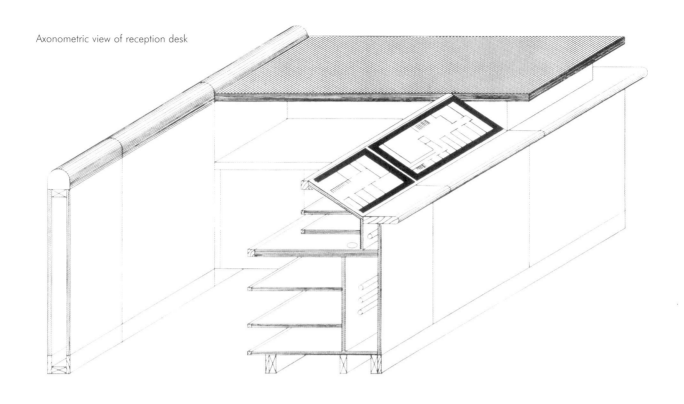

Axonometric view of reception desk

CIBIC & PARTNERS

I.Net Headquarters

PHOTOGRAPHS: SANTI CALECA   **Milan, Italy**

These Milan headquarters for the Internet services supplier, I.Net Group, were deliberately designed to avoid any physical representation of company functioning and performance. The architects, Cibic & Partners, developed various workspace and divider layouts, using degrees of transparency and colored opacity. The starting point in establishing the unique character of the office space was achieved also through the use of special floors and ceilings to contain systems. The 21,000 m² industrial building has six floors and each one is a sequence of fluid, dynamic, multicolored environments, small autonomous 'places' in their own right, intended to elicit emotional engagement by using unexpected situations to stimulate the senses and the imagination. The entry court is austerely sculpted and the reception area has a huge glass sheet as its back wall, while the relaxation room with its custom-made seats, table and chairs is an appropriately playful experience, and the cool minimalism of the stainless steel and white glass bar area is almost glacial.

The entrance can be considered the heart of the internal space of the ground floor. Two interconnected wings expand around the two central areas, which cover the six floors and where services and the elevator landing are located. The so-called "technological" room is also on the ground floor, housing the central and electrical systems. The Web Farm consists of laboratories situated on the four central levels of the building. This space was created through the use of foldable partitions in double-paned shatterproof glass.

Ground floor plan

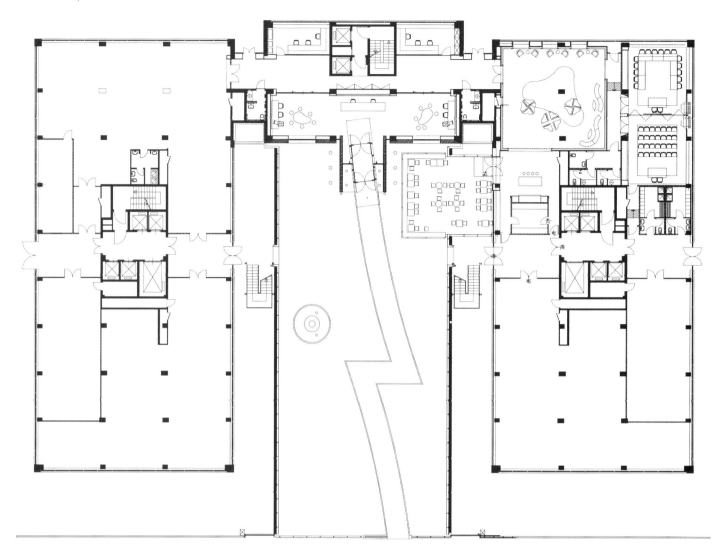

First floor plan

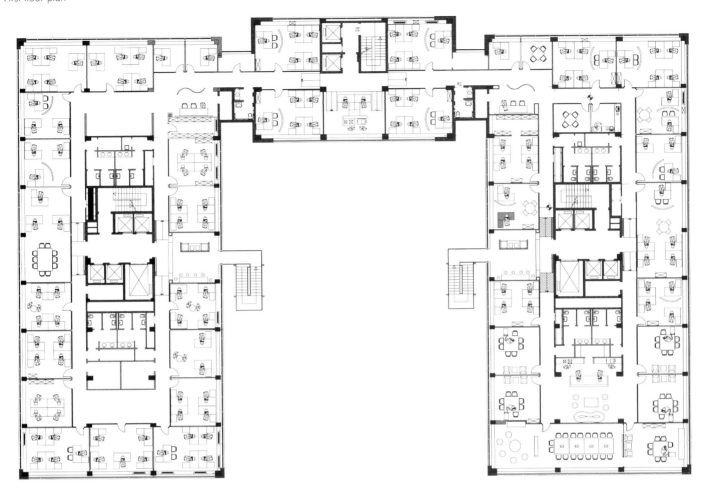

On either side of the entrance hall are two small glass-partitioned waiting rooms equipped with internet access points and furnished with Moroso 'Saruyama' sofas and Kartell 'Moorea' chairs. An acid-green colored wall hides the photocopier area as well as the elevators.

DENYS & VON AREND +
GUY SONET

Renault Design Barcelona

PHOTOGRAPHS: JOAN MUNDÓ

Barcelona, Spain

The aim of this commission was to create a favorable environment where the company's design team could carry out its creative work, while conserving the industrial feel of the building.

The solution proposed has been a combination of pure lines, clear spaces and soft colors with bare brick walls, double heights, exposed installations, and metal and glass enclosures.

One of the key resources has been the treatment of light and color. The lighting of each space is designed to subtly magnify the contrast between the elegant shapes, simple brickwork and steel enclosures. The color blue recurs repeatedly and is lit up and reflected in ceilings and glass faces, introducing a discordant note into the general harmony.

Another of the important elements of the project has been the creation of warm, comfortable, almost homelike spaces that are more reminiscent of a home workshop than an office.

The entrance works as a multi-purpose open space, presided over by the library, and with a rest area furnished like a living room.

Using the existing pillars, the ground floor is divided into two spaces by a row of large cupboard-blocks that separate the work area (on the façade side) from the reception and presentation area (on the courtyard side). Finally, the meeting room and executive office are closed off by a glass screen, in front of which has been placed an iron screen.

Floor plan

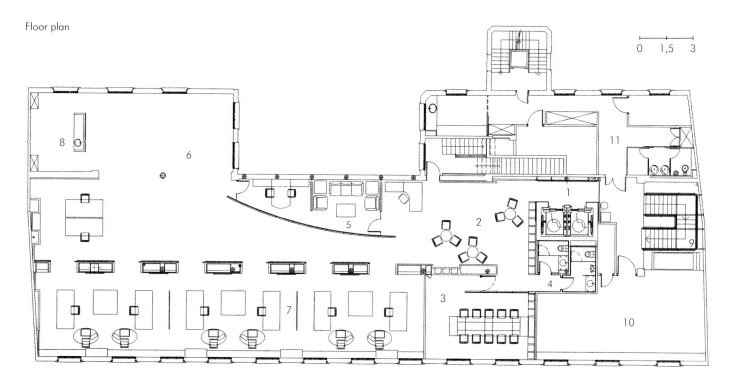

1. Hall
2. Reception-Library
3. Meeting room
4. Bathroom
5. Manager's office
6. Presentation room

7. Design room
8. Storage
9. Stairway
10. Layout workshop
11. General services

Interior courtyard

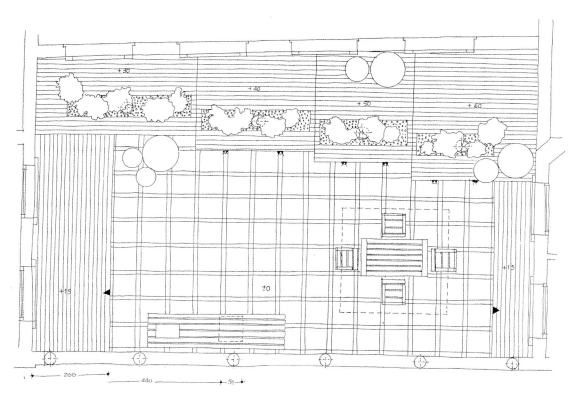

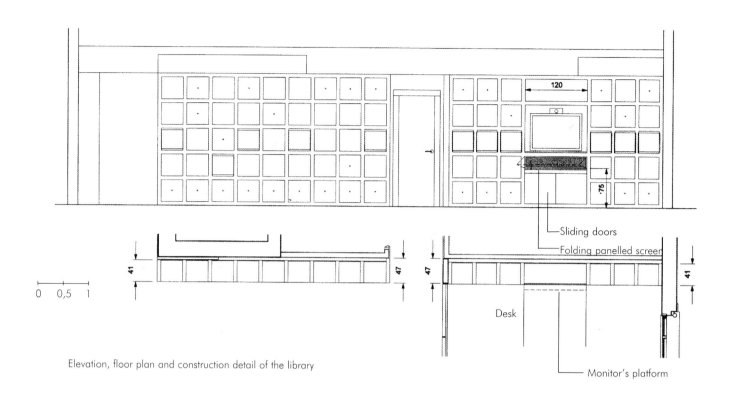

120

·75

Sliding doors

Folding panelled screen

41   47   47   41

Desk

0   0,5   1

Monitor's platform

Elevation, floor plan and construction detail of the library

Section   Elevation

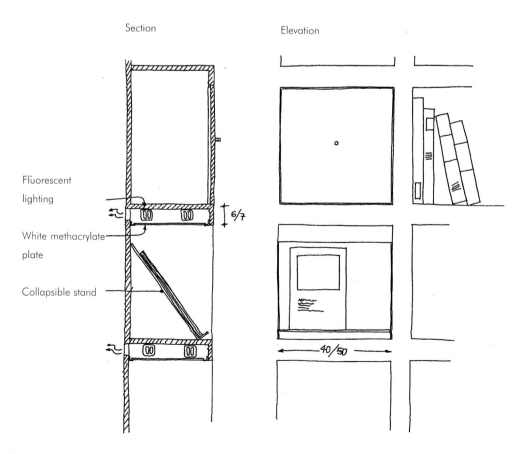

Fluorescent
lighting

6/7

White methacrylate
plate

Collapsible stand

40/50

In order to create a greater sense of space, the areas have been divided with glass and steel Oxidón-treated partitions and arranged in a meticulous interplay of volumes. For example, the large cupboard-block covered by the bulletin board separates the design area from the presentation room.

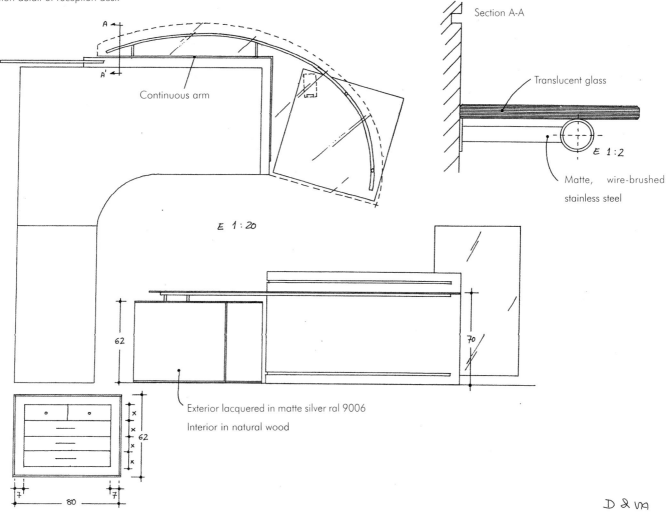

Section A-A

Continuous arm

Translucent glass

E 1:20

E 1:2

Matte, wire-brushed
stainless steel

62

70

Exterior lacquered in matte silver ral 9006

Interior in natural wood

62

7   80   7

D & VA

Construction detail of management desk

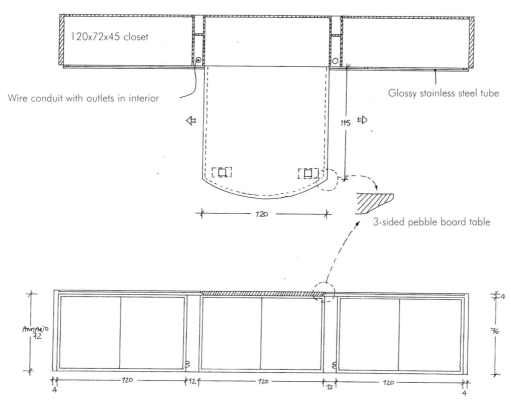

120x72x45 closet

Glossy stainless steel tube

Wire conduit with outlets in interior

115

120

3-sided pebble board table

Armario
72

76   4

4   120   12   120   12   120   4

Construction detail of video conference room

Floor plan   Wire conduit   Sketch   Natural wood

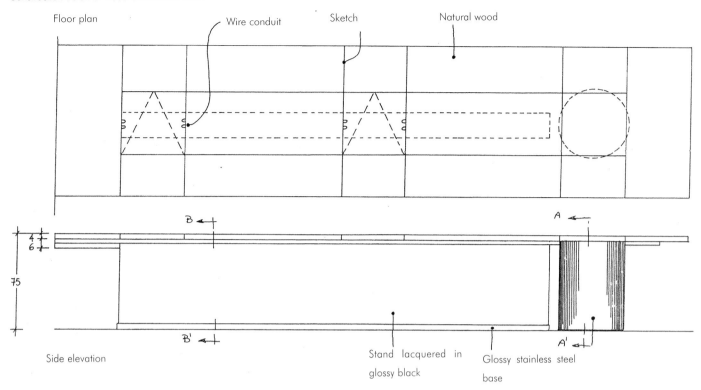

Side elevation

B ◄   A ◄
B' ◄   A' ◄

75   4   6

Stand lacquered in
glossy black

Glossy stainless steel
base

Construction detail of Rimón table

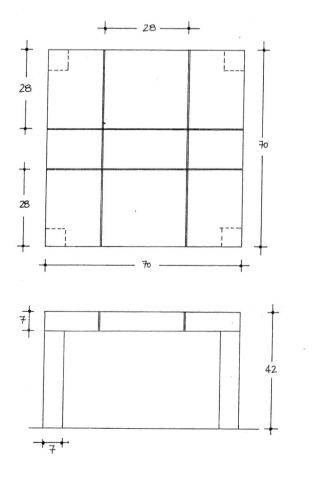

28   28

28   28

70

70

7   7

42

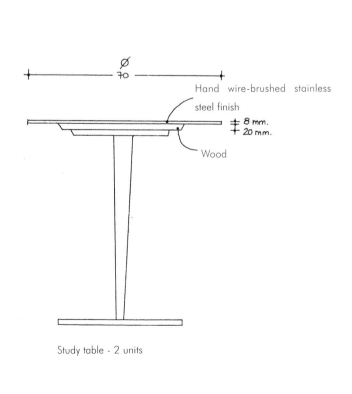

Ø
70

Hand wire-brushed stainless
steel finish

8 mm.
20 mm.

Wood

Study table - 2 units

The service elevator, located next to the stairs, is enclosed in a sand-treated glass box and illuminated in blue. This latter resource recurs repeatedly in ceilings and glass faces with the idea of introducing a discordant note into the general harmony.

The Segurit glass used in the bathrooms is acid etched with fillets, and lets light through while maintaining privacy.

Bathroom section

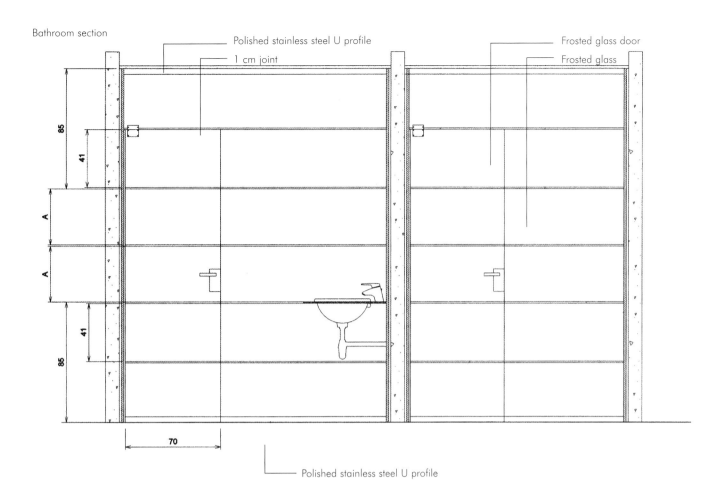

Polished stainless steel U profile
1 cm joint
Frosted glass door
Frosted glass

85
41
A
A
41
85

70

Polished stainless steel U profile

Herzog & de Meuron

Ricola Marketing Building

Photographs: Margherita Spiluttini

Laufen, Switzerland

The new building is located in the middle of a group of small-scale village buildings without any remarkable architectural qualities. The surrounding gardens, however, with their hedges and trees, offered a wonderful environment for a transparent architecture relating the interior and exterior spaces.

Instead of a multi-story volume that would dominate the architectural landscape, the architects chose a low polygonal installation that fits into Ricola's garden area like a pavilion, an architecture in which outer form and geometry did not immediately reveal themselves. One which, thanks to its turned-back facades, dissolves into single pieces. Each piece has the distinct characteristic of either surrounding, reflecting, or projecting far into the building's interior a special site in the garden.

The deep cantilevered roof can be understood as a symbol for the strategy utilised here of melting nature and architecture. Roof beams are made of a special plastic having variable flexibility for assimilation to changing temperatures and the changing weight of rain or snow. Plants, woven among the beams, form a hybrid natural-artificial construction which lends the building an ever-changing appearance in accordance with the passing seasons. Ivy provides for basic green throughout the year between the beams. The leaves of other plants - wild vine, for example- are only visible during the summer months and help to prevent too much sun from penetrating the glass facades.

Inside, the building is planned as a single, cohesive, open space that offers, for the most part, a transparent office landscape on two floors. The large staircase in the middle of the building is simultaneously a connecting element, meeting place and auditorium. The building is equipped with facades of pure glass throughout, with a few wall-height sliding doors. Thus actual spatial delineation is not static and may be changed according to need. Curtains mounted on three parallel runners allow users differing variables as to color, transparency and view.

Like its landscape design, the building's textile equipment is indivisibly bound to its architectural concept. In no way is it a more or less coincidental decorative element. Its conception demanded early and close co-operation with the landscape architect Kienast Vogt and with artists Rosmarie Trockel and Adrian Schiess.

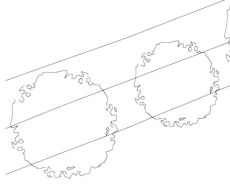

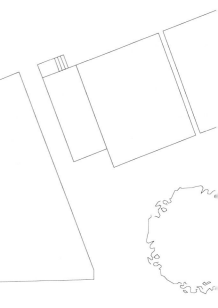

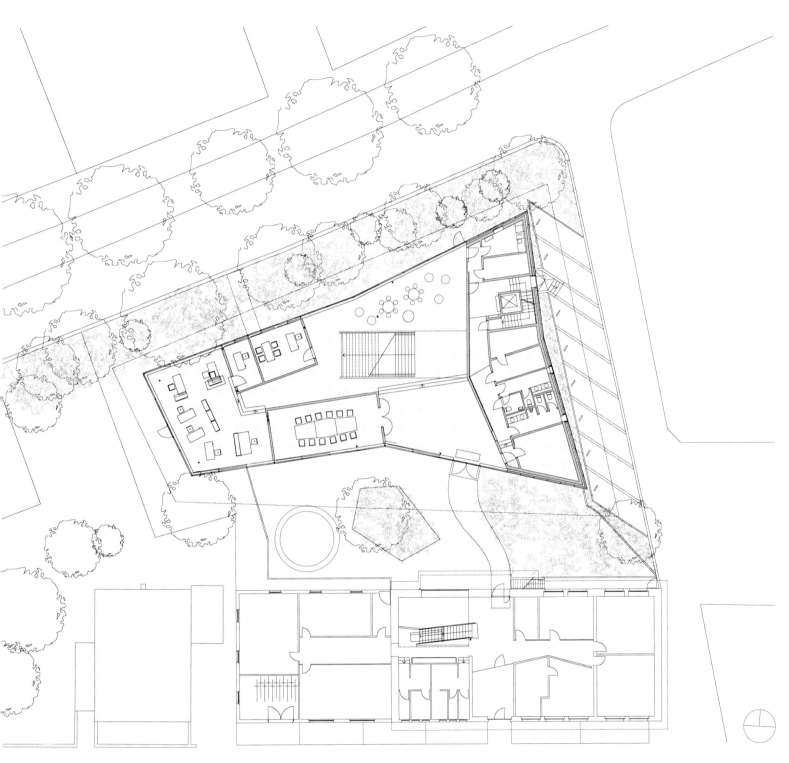

Ground floor plan

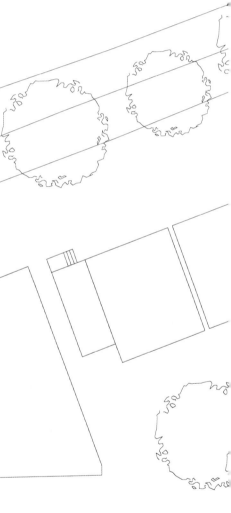

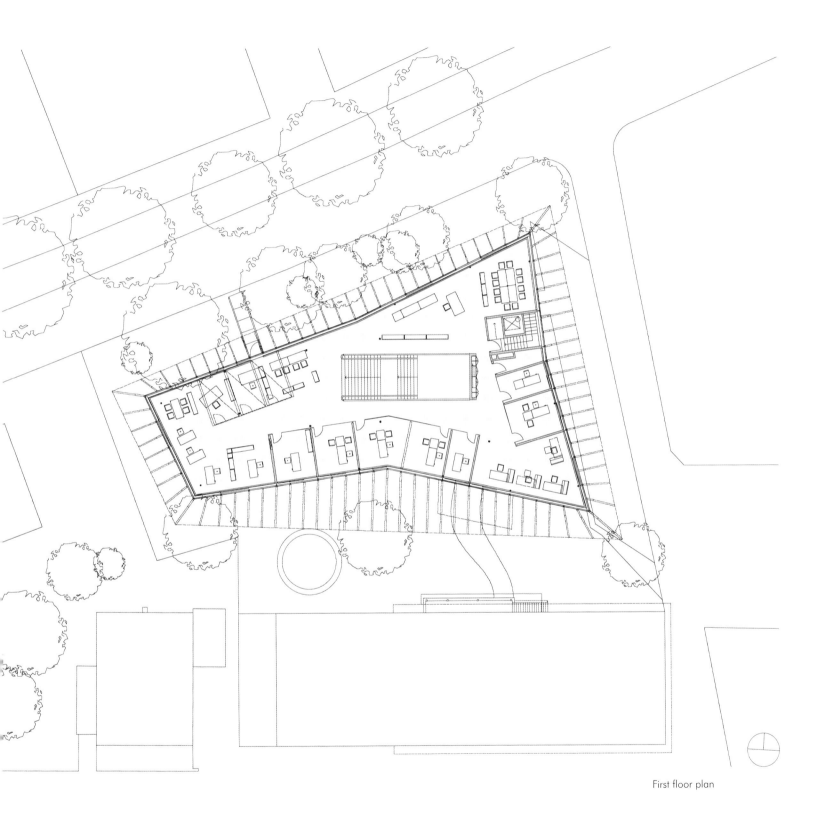

First floor plan

West elevation

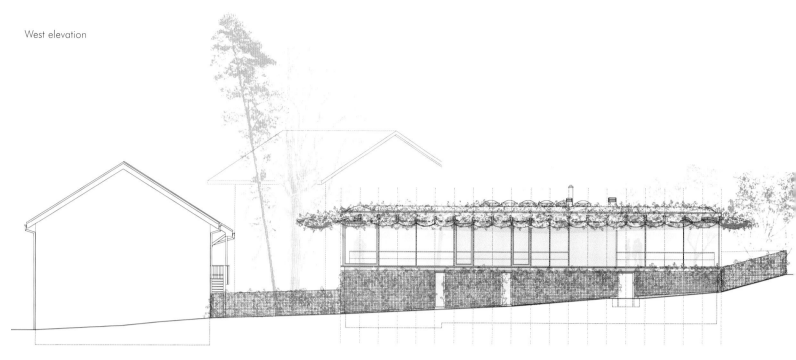

Longitudinal section

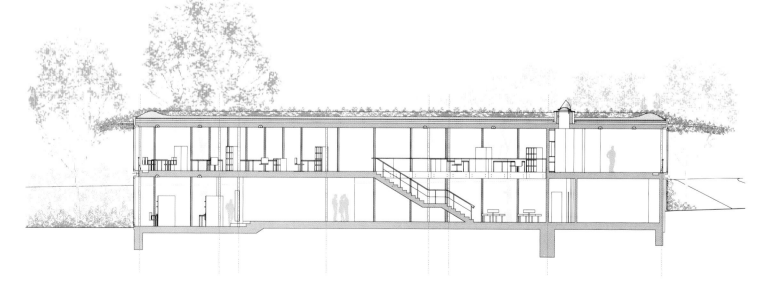

South elevation

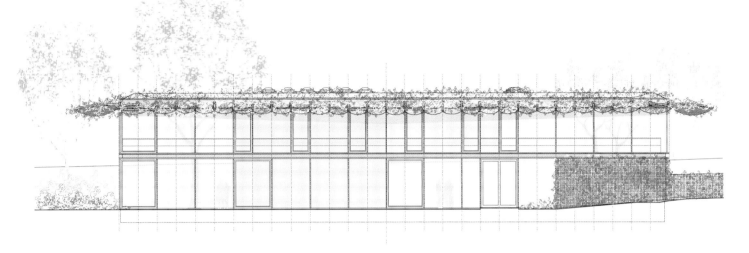

Cross-section

The interior of the building is conceived as a transparent space, with glass divisions that evoke the glazed facade and favor communication between the members of the firm. Three layers of curtains mounted on parallel rails allow an interplay between variables of color, light and views.

PRIESTMAN ARCHITECTS

Ted Baker Headquarters

PHOTOGRAPHS: DAVID GLANDORGE

London, UK

Witty and inventive, these London head offices for the fashion design company, Ted Baker plc, creatively recolonize a former post office building.

Matthew Preistman Architects were commissioned to remodel the 40,000 sq ft premises. A conventional mixture of offices, meeting rooms, showrooms and a staff canteen was required, but these also had to reflect the underlying informal philosophy of the company.

The entry is signposted by a huge lobster billboard, an instant graphic landmark. The route to the upper levels is animated by a linear history of Ted Baker displays. Existing elevator cages go up to the third-floor reception area, revealing the spectacular interiors.

The central, triangular courtyard has been covered with a glazed roof to add space and light. Configured around the courtyard, the second and third floors are large open-plan areas for showrooms, workstations and meeting rooms. Stairs lead down from the office level to the lower floor. The staff canteen occupies the center of the courtyard, surrounded by bands of showrooms enclosed by sliding canvas and stainless-steel screens. The original canal-side cladding has been replaced with glazed sliding doors that lead on to cedar-clad balconies.

The building has been stripped back to its bare shell, with exposed sandblasted structures. The existing concrete floor screed has been sealed, with traces of the original floor surfaces and partitions still faintly visible. All building services are routed from the ceiling or perimeter walls, so that workspaces can be adapted to individual needs.

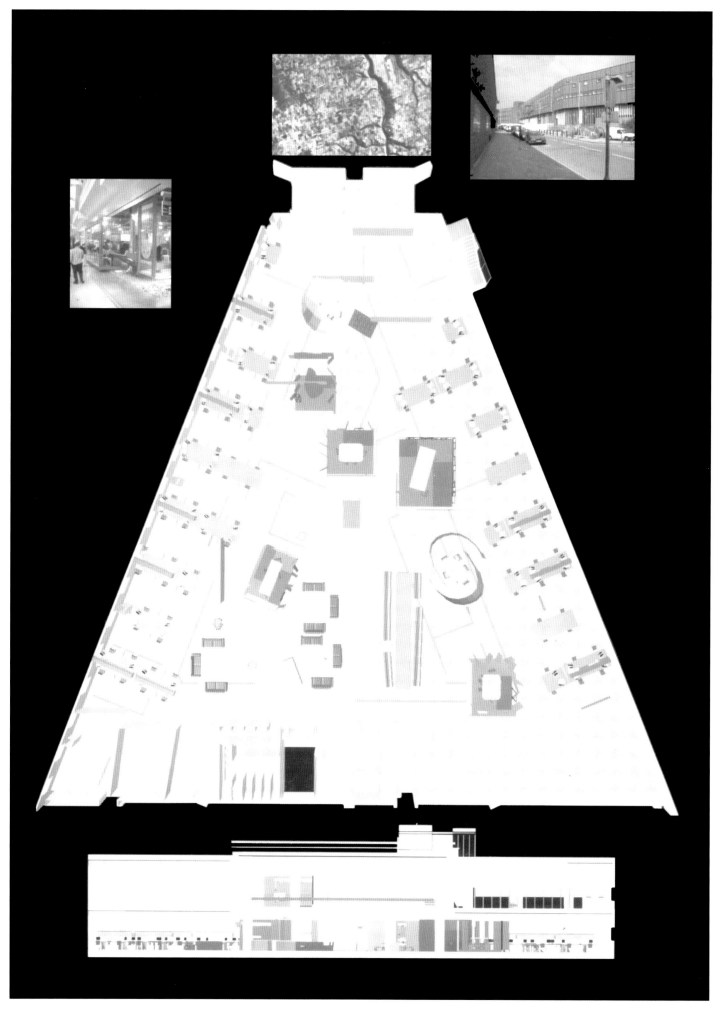

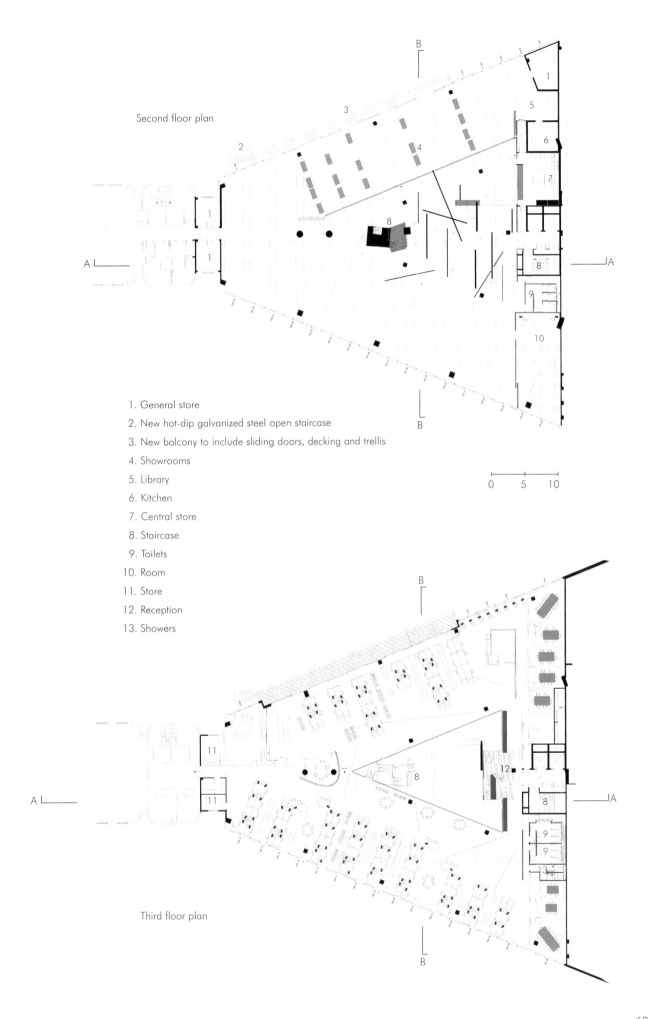

Second floor plan

1. General store
2. New hot-dip galvanized steel open staircase
3. New balcony to include sliding doors, decking and trellis
4. Showrooms
5. Library
6. Kitchen
7. Central store
8. Staircase
9. Toilets
10. Room
11. Store
12. Reception
13. Showers

0   5   10

Third floor plan

Section BB

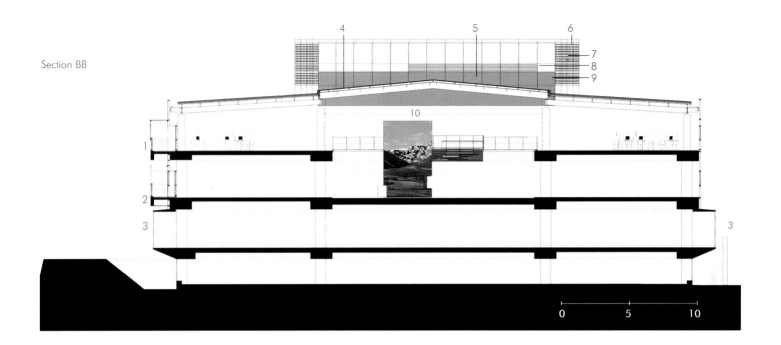

Section AA

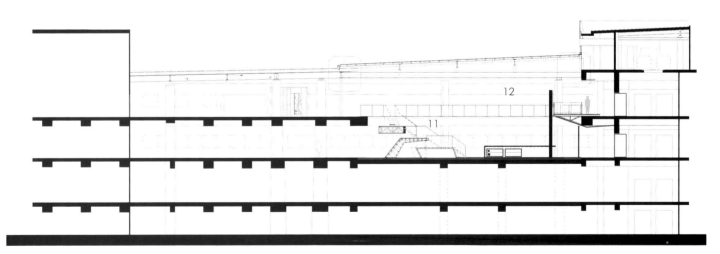

1. Cedar slatting rails, trellis and shading to existing
   and proposed balcony
2. New balcony
3. New glazing by freeholder
4. New glazed roof to courtyard
5. New replacement cladding to front
6. Approximately 12 m2 of aluminum louvers to M&E
   specification; design and quantity to M&E specification.

7. New grills
8. Existing grills
9. Shaded section
10. Double height wall
11. Staircase
12. Reception

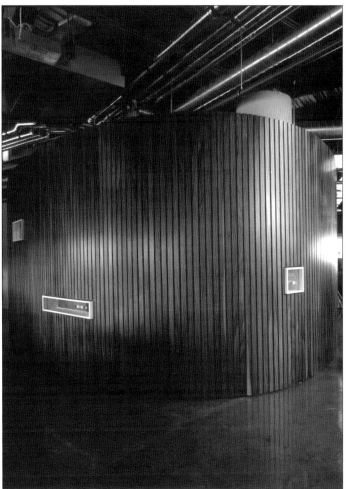

40,000 ft² head offices for retailer Ted Baker plc, with reception areas, show-rooms, meeting rooms, a staff canteen and extensive alterations to the external fabric, including atrium glazing, of the former postal sorting office. The outside of the building facing the street is unaltered, whilst the interiors are open, creative and forward-thinking. Quirky, yet with an inventive approach to materials and space handling, this makeover seeks to crystallize the company's philosophy.

GCA ARQUITECTES ASSOCIATS

Architecture Studio

PHOTOGRAPHS: JORDI MIRALLES

Barcelona, Spain

The office of GCA Arquitectes, located in the Eixample (19th-century new development area) of Barcelona, was converted from a textile warehouse. The scheme, by the architects themselves, takes advantage of the original structure of the property and creates a transparent, clear and homogenous space in which the lighting is a key element. The premises had a rectangular ground plan and a floor area of 1000 sqm. It was divided into two areas: the front, used for the offices and the rear, used for the warehouse. The intervention of GCA respected the original layout, which became the main reference of the scheme.

For the entrance, the initial premise was to recover the original image, restoring door and window frames and providing it with the necessary facilities for the reception and the administration and project management offices. The interior area, on the other hand, with a free and transparent floor plan supported by riveted metal trusses and pillars, was conceived as a modern environment, a large white box housing a sequence of spaces for designing and managing projects, all of which culminates in an inner courtyard.

In this area devoted to the creative process the lighting is particularly important and is achieved naturally thanks to two large skylights that provide pleasant top lighting. As a complement, light fixtures were suspended from the ceiling, in addition to spotlights on tracks and indirect lighting elements such as the Tolomeo lamp by Artemide.

With the intention of forming a homogenous, neutral and minimalist atmosphere of imprecise limits and multiple visions and perspectives, a limited selection of materials was used (maple wood, glass, aluminum and deco-metal), with solutions that favor visual continuity: large glass screens, wooden floors in all the spaces and white walls. Most of the furniture is the work of GCA and follows the same minimalist parameters as the scheme. It was supplemented with selected elements.

The interior is prolonged toward the exterior. A vertical glass wall separates the studio from the inner courtyard. The connection between closed and open spaces is multiplied thanks to the deck of the courtyard that merges with the wooden floor of the studio.

The system of skylights infuses the space with natural light while also greatly increasing the visual perception of space.

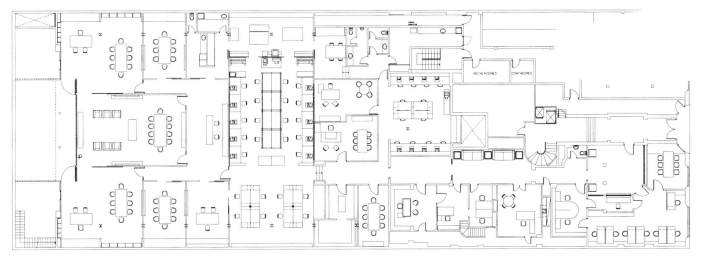

General floor plan

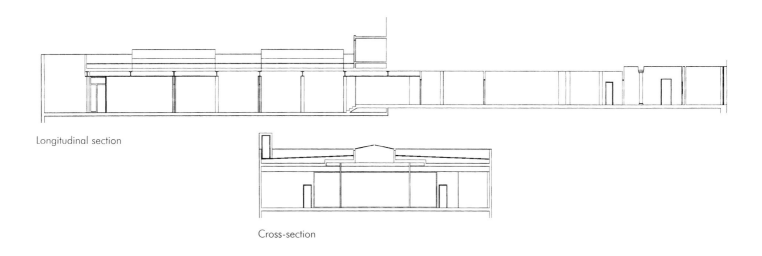

Longitudinal section

Cross-section

In the area devoted to project management, under the inner courtyard, a series of transparent spaces was created, reinforced by natural lighting through skylights. The warmth of the wooden floor contrasts with industrial elements such as the beams that support the glass roof or the light fixtures that hang from the ceiling.

HAH
AGNETA HAHNE ARKITEKTER AB

Peer Communication AB

PHOTOGRAPHS: ÅKE E:SON LINDMAN

Malmö, Sweden

The office of the Peer Eriksson advertising agency dates from the sixties. It was a former bank that was dull and lacking light, like the surrounding buildings, but after the conversion it stands bright and shining, in clear contrast to its environment. The facade that now gives access to the agency was transformed very audaciously: in the reception area, behind the high narrow windows of the facade, a wall rises catching the eye of the passers-by and making them wonder what must go on inside the building.

Behind the wall of the reception there is a white corridor with narrow glass windows that reflect the proportions of the facade openings. These proportions are coherently maintained throughout the whole space. The accounts department is on one side of this corridor, with two meeting rooms on the opposite side. The clients never go beyond this point, since the agency must respect the confidentiality of their clients' business. The corridor opens up to a large bright studio with a high ceiling, where natural light penetrates through the skylights and the glazed dome of the original construction. The large rear wall is used to display the current projects, facilitating the exchange of ideas between the creative staff. A second wall also facilitates the exchange of ideas, although in a different way: it is the location for a table where the staff of the company meet to eat, have coffee and inspire each other. The original vault of the bank and the stone wall have been conserved. This small room houses Peer Eriksson's pride and joy: the archive of the agency. A very uniform and homogenous space has been achieved thanks to the orderly layout of the spaces and the use of simple materials: varnished beech wood, steel and glass.

While natural light floods the work area, the other areas are lit by lamps fitted into the ceiling that increase the sensation of space. Agneta Hahne's personal touch is shown in each detail of the project: she was responsible for designing all the furniture, with the exception of the chairs and the waste paper bins, which come from David Design. Each employee has the same furniture: a desk and a small beech wood auxiliary unit on wheels. The furniture is light and flexible, very appropriate for a transparent work area in which all members of the agency have their own space.

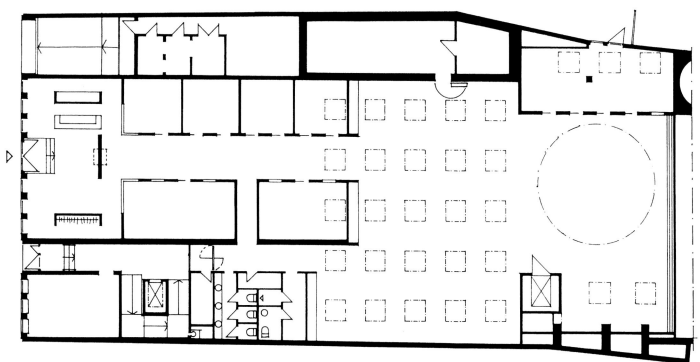

Floor plan

Longitudinal section

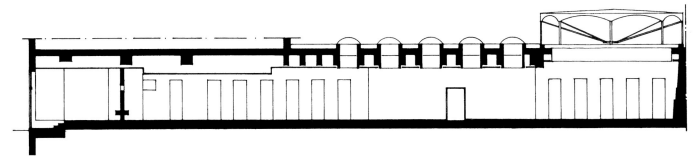

Harmony of space, light and color are the project's main characteristics. The new facade has been shaped with artistic integrity, making it a distinctive feature of this Malmö backstreet. The left hand wall of the reception area conceals a cloakroom, fax and photocopier. It is effectively screened from view creating curiosity and expectations.

The glass dome and skylights have been preserved from the building's previous life. The existing ceiling dome dictated the lighting scheme. All employees have an identical work table and rolling cupboard in beech wood. These, like the rest of the furnishing, were specially designed.

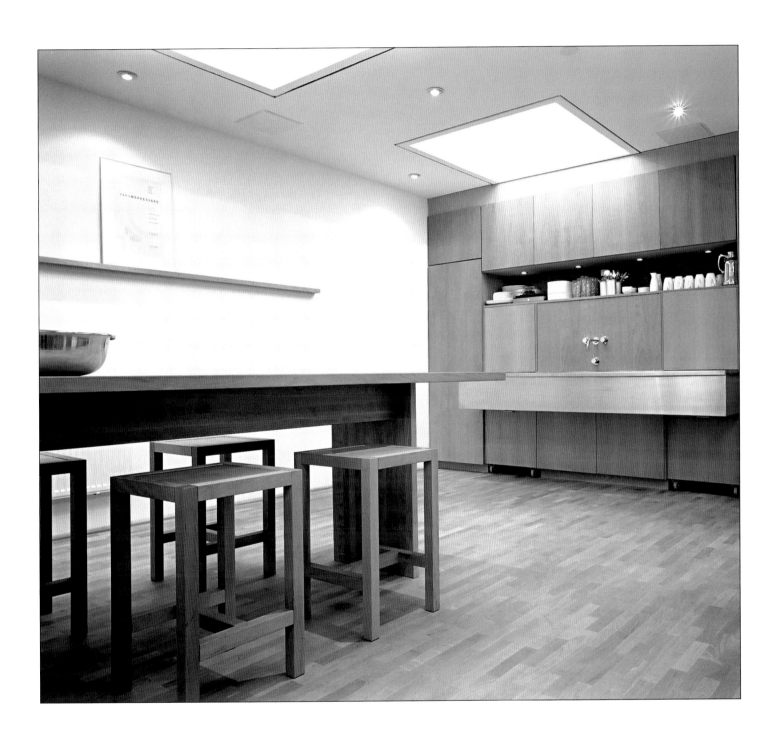

MARMOL RADZINER AND ASSOCIATES

TBWA\Chiat\Day Offices

PHOTOGRAPHS: BENNY CHAN/FOTOWORKS

San Francisco, USA

Marmol Radziner and Associates received the commission to renovate an 85-year-old four-story warehouse near the San Francisco Bay for the advertising firm of TBWA \ Chiat \ Day. The architects sought inspiration for the design in the site's maritime history, and the architectural forms and materials are a reference to the ships buried beneath the building as well as the cargo crates stored in the former warehouse.

By stripping the building down to its existing brick walls, wood ceilings, timber columns and large glass windows, the space and access to natural light are significantly improved.

A huge, upward curving wall of rough horizontal boards, recalling a fragment of a wooden ship's outer hull, draws visitors through the lobby. The upper floor has been cut away to reveal other curving laminated forms, which suggest the ribs of oddly configured ships. Only partially visible overhead, these elements form the structure of translucent polycarbonate-lined conference and project rooms on the second level.

In special areas, such as a lounge, the floor is covered in cork, while elsewhere floor cladding is sealed, construction-grade plywood. The two floors of office space follow mostly an open plan, where custom-built plywood stations stand in neat orthogonal rows.

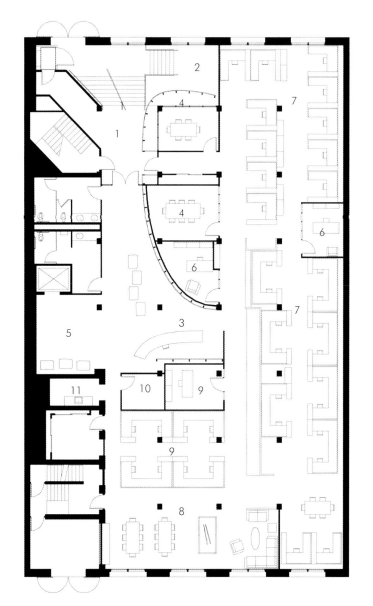

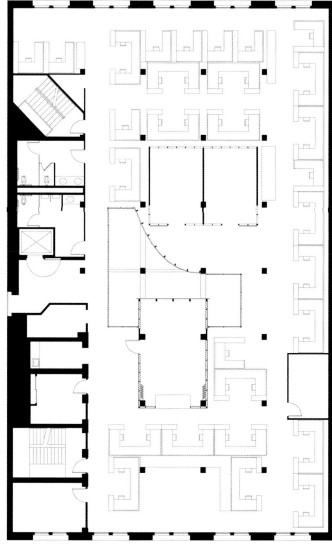

Ground floor

First floor

1. Entrance
2. Void
3. Reception
4. Meeting
5. Elevator lobby
6. Office
7. Workstations
8. Play area
9. Production
10. Viewing
11. Kitchen

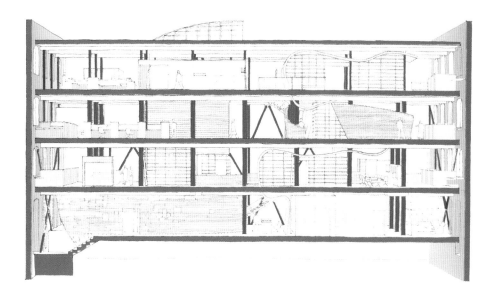

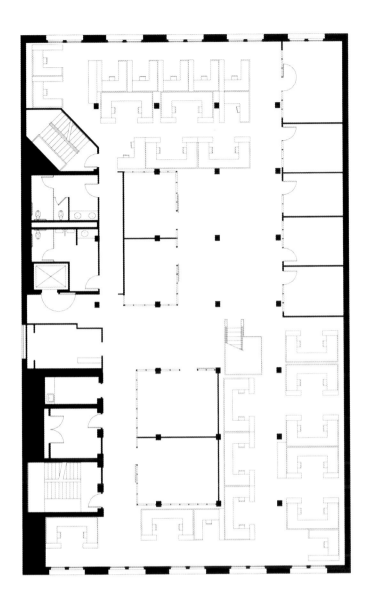

Second floor

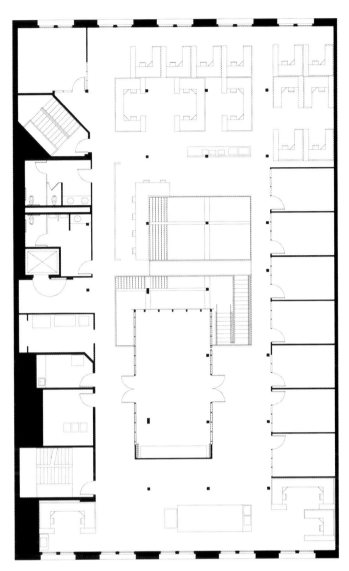

Third floor

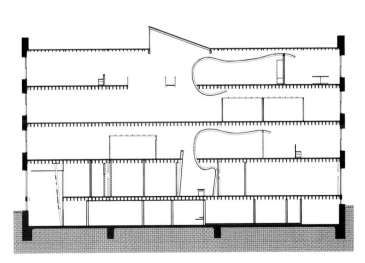

KAUFFMANN THEILIG & PARTNER FREIE ARCHITEKTEN BDA

Werdich Headquarter Offices

PHOTOGRAPHS: ROLAND HALBE /ARTUR

Dornstadt, Germany

Built in the 1970's and guided by functional and economical criteria, Werdich's central offices consisted of a ground floor building and a separate warehouse, built with prefabricated sections of reinforced concrete. Company growth forced the office surface to be extended about 2,000 m², giving the buildings their own identity.

The extension consisted of a new three-story block between the office building and the existing warehouse: a curved, wooden shell inclined upwards with large glass panels.

The external part of the building's shell represents a visible company feature, as well as being the main entrance to the building. It is formed by aluminum tubes that act as parasols and filter the view of the adjacent blacktop roofs.

In the lower part, a large communicative space connects the different levels of offices. Among other services, this building accommodates meeting rooms and small staff cafeterias, an elevator and glazed staircases.

The rectangular openings in the shell have been optimized from the technical point of view of lighting, providing daily light to the three levels of offices and balconies.

As regards the location, the site is on Lerchenbergstrasse, with sweeping views to the south. The other views are limited by very heterogenous industrial buildings and by the state highway. The construction available forced the projection of an architectural body facing longitudinally from east to west, with the offices facing north and south, towards the jumbled flat roofs of the adjacent industrial buildings.

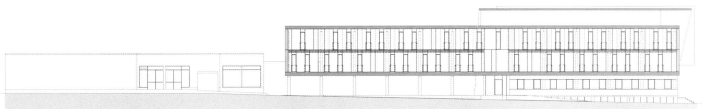

West elevation

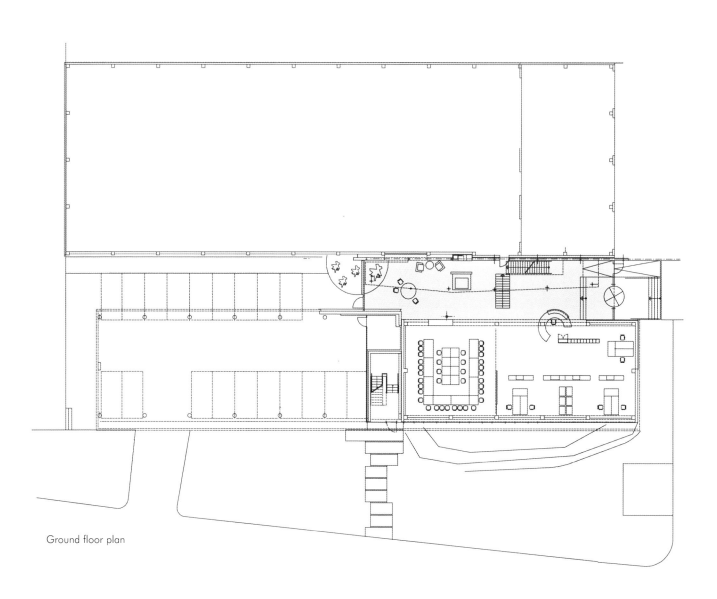

Ground floor plan

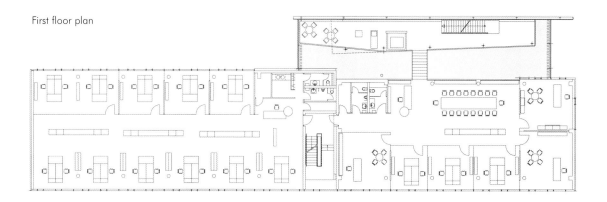

First floor plan

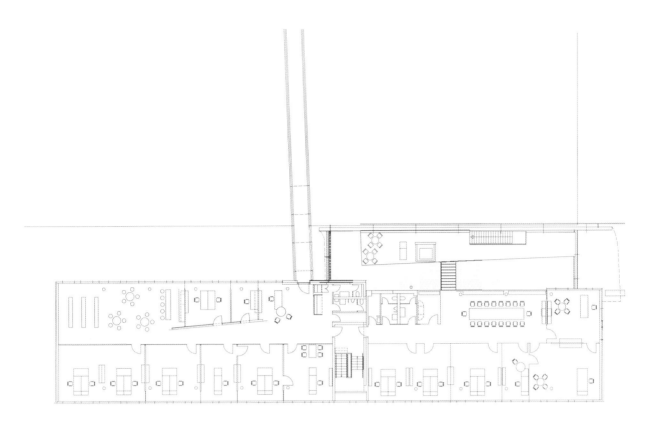

Second floor plan

Cross section

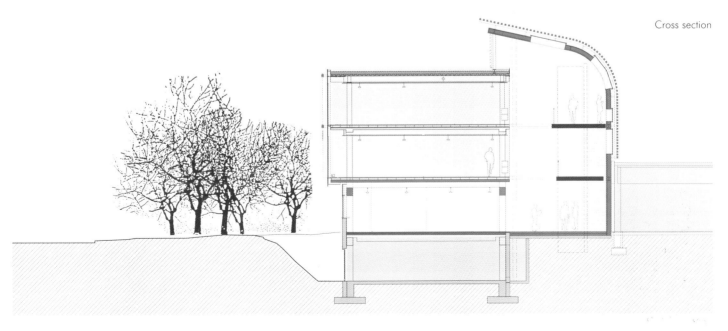

Depending on their use, the different floors can be converted into space for individual offices, for groups or as a large open-plan space. The versatile and full-length glazed separating walls act as an acoustic barrier as well as offering the necessary transparency. All of this generates an open and communicative office space, completely focussed on satisfying user requirements.

Schmidt, Hammer & Lassen

Nykredit Headquarters

PHOTOGRAPHS: JØRGEN TRUE AND SØREN KUHN

Copenhagen, Denmark

Danish practice Schmidt, Hammer & Lassen's headquarters for Nykredit is by far the finest new building on Copenhagen's waterfront. Seen from the outside, the building is an enormous cube facing the water. Each side is slightly different. One enters from the elevation parallel to the water. The low-ceilinged foyer has an aura of 1960's glamour and spectacular pieces by artists Per Kierkeby and Anita Jørgensen line the reception area.

Stairs lead up to the first floor to enter the principal atrium. The company's 300-seat cafeteria is located on this floor. Suspended in the air above are walkways linking the upper floors and wenge-clad meeting 'boxes' that project out into the atrium void. From here, the two blocks of office accommodation are clearly visible. These are all laid out according to a 'new way of working' philosophy, with open plans, glass boxes for quiet work and flexible wiring. Management suites and the accounts department are separately located on the two platforms spanning the atrium at a high level.

By raising the main atrium space one floor above street level, using the low reception as a buffer zone, the architect has overcome the problematic presence of the main road outside.

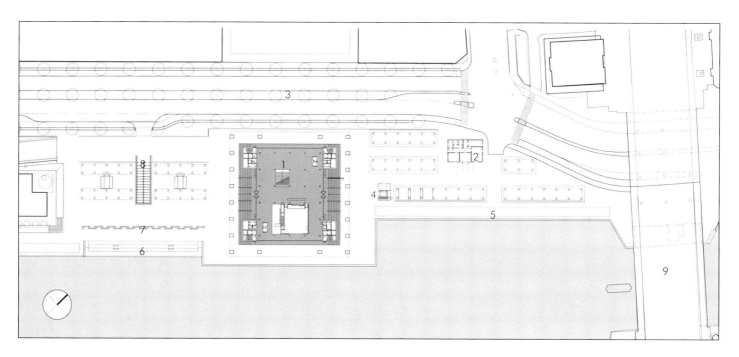

Site plan

1. Nykredit - New Headquarters
2. Toldbygningen (former Customs House)
3. Kalvedbod Brygge
4. Service building

5. Promenade
6. Water stairs
7. Stone ornament by Per Kierkeby
8. Ramp to parking area
9. Langebro

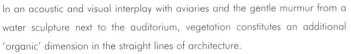

In an acoustic and visual interplay with aviaries and the gentle murmur from a water sculpture next to the auditorium, vegetation constitutes an additional 'organic' dimension in the straight lines of architecture.

Under the large round skylights, the atrium connects the open and flexible eight-story administration areas of the two flanking office sections. Suspended 'meeting boxes' sided with dark wenge wood create a dynamic effect in the bright atrium, accentuating the meeting room as an important common function.

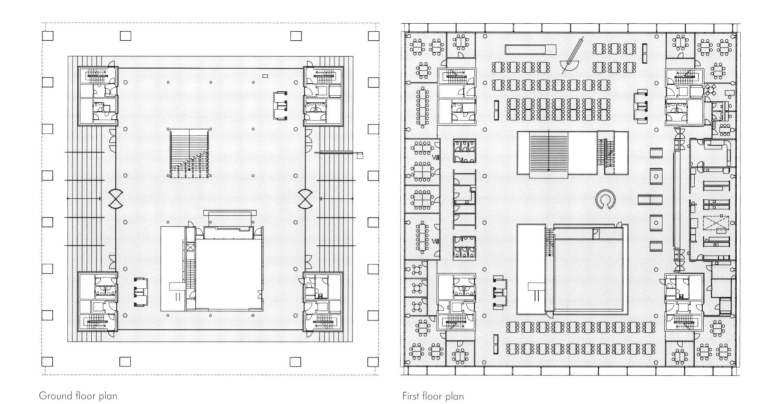

Ground floor plan   First floor plan

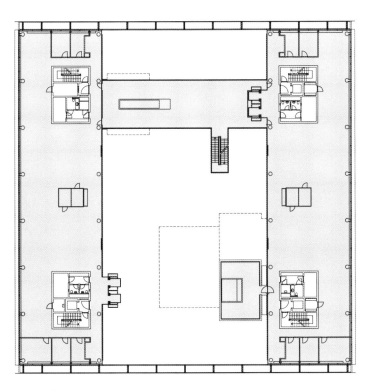

Seventh floor plan

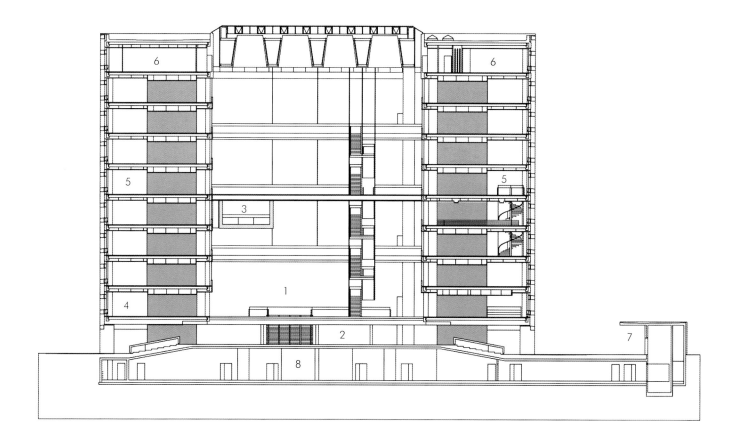

1. Atrium, canteen
2. Lobby, entrance
3. Meeting box
4. Meeting section
5. Open office space
6. Management floor
7. Service building
8. Basement

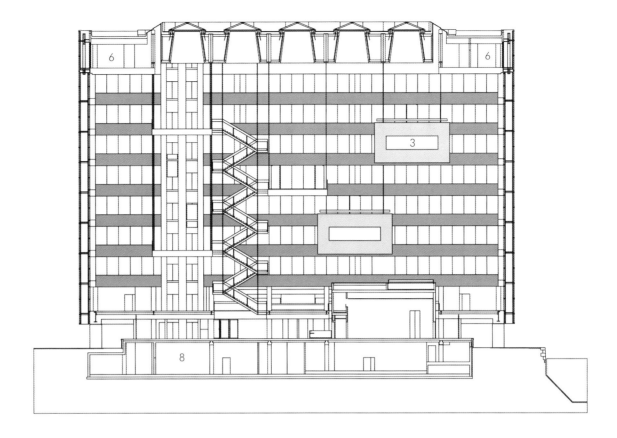

The meeting rooms, which have been designed as boxes, are fastened to the rows of columns, and – with built-in vibration absorbers – suspended from the roof or footbridges. A wide stairway rises in a combination of lightweight and transparency as well as monumentality from the entrance floor towards the light and drama of the atrium.

SIDNAM PETRONE GARTNER ARCHITECTS

NYC Offices of America On Line

PHOTOGRAPHS: MICHAEL MORAN

New York, USA

The scheme for the offices of America On Line, designed by Sidnam/Petrone, combines simplicity, functionality and lyricism. The activity of the company conditioned the spirit of the design: physical presence, proximity and interaction. The space was articulated following two guidelines: communication and versatility. A large central forum would act as a meeting place for the employees and the clients, and a space for presentations and leisure activities. The possibility of making future changes in the distribution of the elements was also a requirement. The third decisive factor was the limited budget. The objective was to demonstrate that the company would rather invest in services than in the creation of an expensive corporate image.

The space, of almost 1500 sq m, is divided into two areas, public and private, each of which can be illuminated or darkened thanks to the combination of the lighting systems and the construction materials. Two slightly curved walls with a coffered wooden structure clad in perforated metal panels conceal the offices and the work tables from the view of the clients and visitors. Thanks to the curved contours, according to the ever-changing lighting conditions the panels that act as walls appear opaque or transparent.

When they started the conversion, the architects found a greenhouse that extended about 30 meters from the frame of the building to the elevator and was not part of the original structure. This volume could not be incorporated into the main structure. For the moment, it has been conserved as a circulation space, reinforced and clad with translucent Lumasite panels.

The offices were distributed around a 7.3 meter high atrium, as if it were a forum. This almost circular distribution of the work space favors visual contact between the members of the company. An original spiral staircase that formerly led to a water tank has also been clad in silver-finish metal plate. This staircase now leads to a room for informal meetings that enjoys extraordinary views of the city.

In the conversion the parquet was replaced, structural modifications were made, a new heating, ventilation and air conditioning system was installed and the electrical installation was replaced.

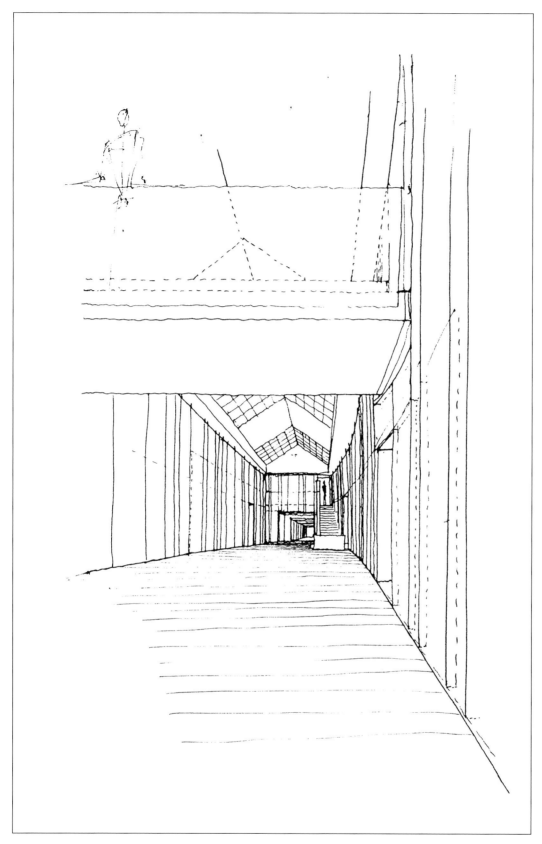

View looking east through main space

In the atrium the architects designed two gently curved wood frame walls faced on one side with perforated metal panels. Because these walls are always at a slight angle when viewed from the atrium space they obscure the office operations from visitors and clients as they enter the space.

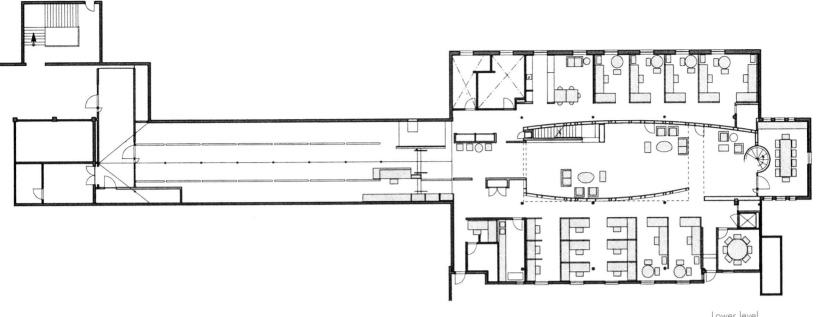

Lower level

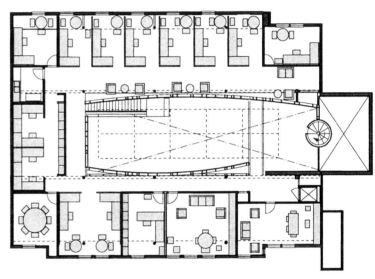

Mezzanine

East-west long section

Cross sections

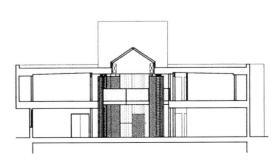

View from the stairs to the southeast

The materials used in the conversion reinforce the image that it was wished to transmit to the clients: dynamism, proximity and freshness. The combination of wood, glass and metal offers imaginative solutions for a limited budget.

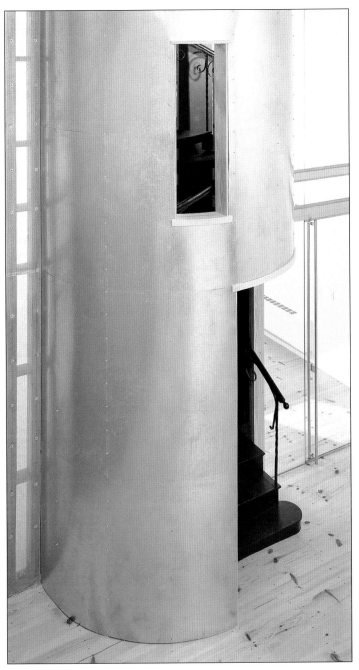

WIEL ARETS

Lensvelt Offices and Warehouse

PHOTOGRAPHS: CHRISTIAN RICHTERS

Breda, Holland

The headquarters of the Dutch transportation company Lensvelt was designed as a single body, a two-story rectangular volume with exterior cladding of folded sheets, interrupted only by the lorry access doors distributed along the facade. The design responded to the company's needs with a homogenous area on the ground floor containing the entrance, the showroom with a loft, the reception area, a patio, a dining room, a shipping office and storage space; while the offices, machine room, dressing room and another storage space are allocated to the first floor.

This building was conceived as a transparent, well-lit, homogenous volume which distances itself from the stereotypical image of industrial constructions, which typically display uniform design with little thought given to aesthetic considerations. The idea was to harmoniously unify, within the same building, the administrative facilities, storage spaces, access for the transport vehicles and service areas.

From the exterior, this building is seen as a partitionless rectangular body with openings for the lorries, whose facade of translucent glass panels casts an abundance of natural light into the interior. Another source of light is the open space which has been left between the walls and the roof, allowing the light to reach even the offices grouped together in the centre of the building. The walls and ceiling, painted white, also contribute to achieving the desired brightness in the building. Wood was used for the flooring and concrete for the vertical faces.

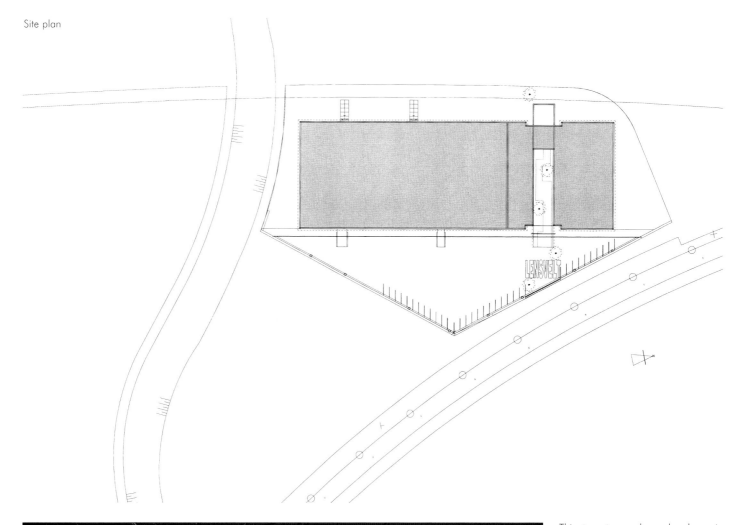

This two-story polygonal volume is perceived as a homogeneous surface without partitions, only interrupted by the access and the lorry bays.

The building has translucent glass facades that provide ample natural lighting.

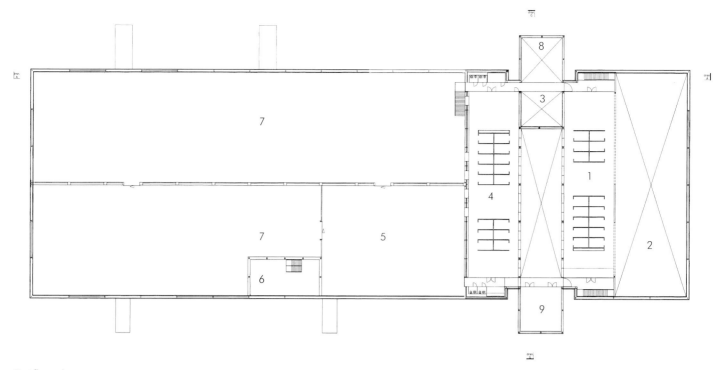

First floor plan

Ground floor plan

1. Showroom
2. Entrance
3. Reception
4. Patio

5. Dining room
6. Dispatch
7. Containers
8. Warehouse
9. Lounge

First floor plan

1. Mezzanine Showroom
2. Void
3. Void
4. Offices

5. Dispatch
6. Utility room
7. Void
8. Void
9. Dressing

Ground floor plan

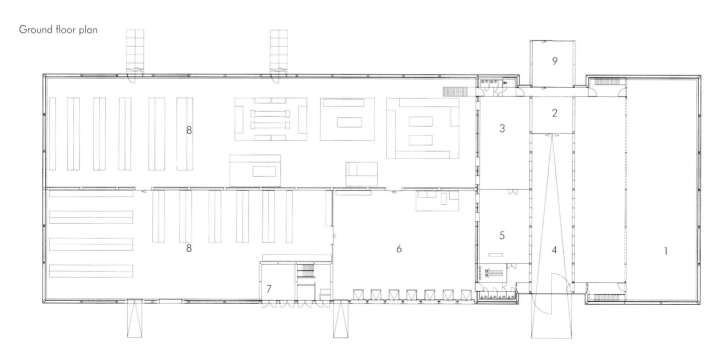

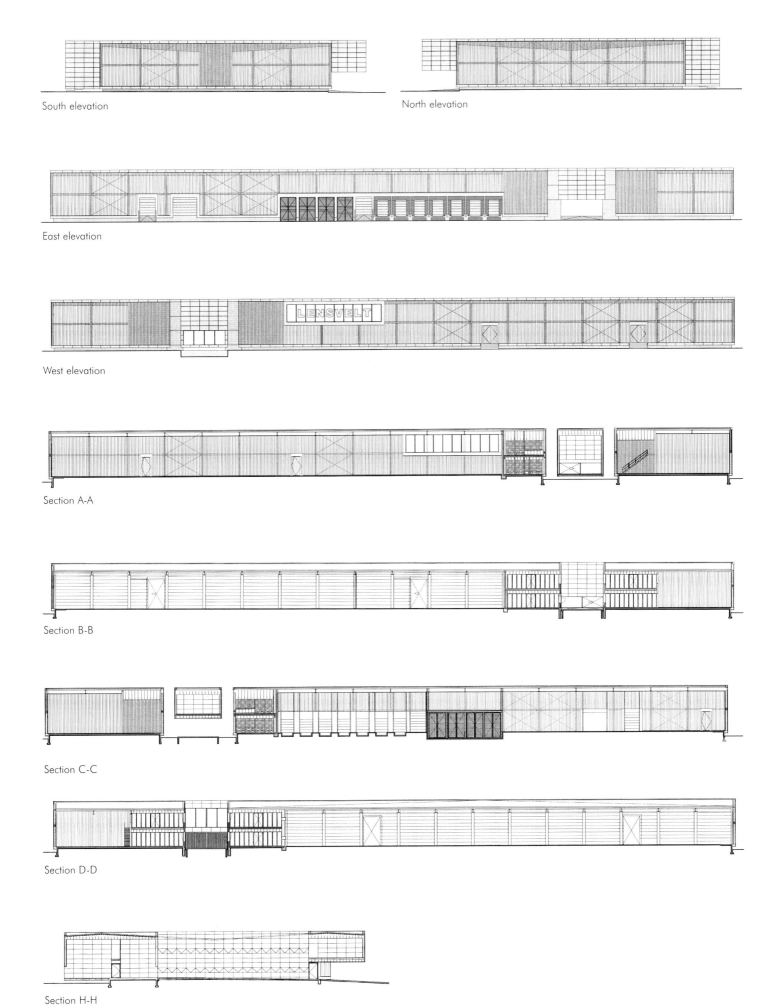

South elevation

North elevation

East elevation

West elevation

Section A-A

Section B-B

Section C-C

Section D-D

Section H-H

133

The free space between the walls and the ceiling lets the light into the offices grouped in the centre of the building. The floor is made of wood and the ceiling and walls are painted white.

WHITE DESIGN
VELUX Sales Office & Training Centre

PHOTOGRAPHS: DAVID CROSS AND WILLMONT DIXON &
WATERHOUSE DESIGN

Kettering, UK

White Design Architects were commissioned to design the new regional sales office and training facility in Kettering, UK for window manufacturer Velux. The client's brief specified that the building was to act as a showcase for Velux products and demonstrate good environmental practice on a commercial basis. This inventive, three-story landmark building with sloping façades functions both as an operational office and as a visitor's center for the public and construction professionals. The innovative program combines high quality design with leading edge technology to minimize energy consumption. Natural cross ventilation and maximum use of daylight ensure increased user comfort and productivity, and reduced energy requirement.

The structure is a timber glue-laminated frame supported by a concrete base at ground and first floor. The roof folds around the main structure, almost touching the ground (slate on one side and cedar shingles on the other). The Velux windows on the upper levels are installed with rain and solar sensors that open and close the windows and blinds.

Inside, White Design has taken its inspiration from the household attic – white walls, sloping roof, warm timber and spiral staircase. At the entrance, an elliptical rotunda acts as an organizing device with stairs wrapped around it and the bridge to the double-height boardroom protruding from it. At the base of the rotunda is a reception that commands the entrance hall.

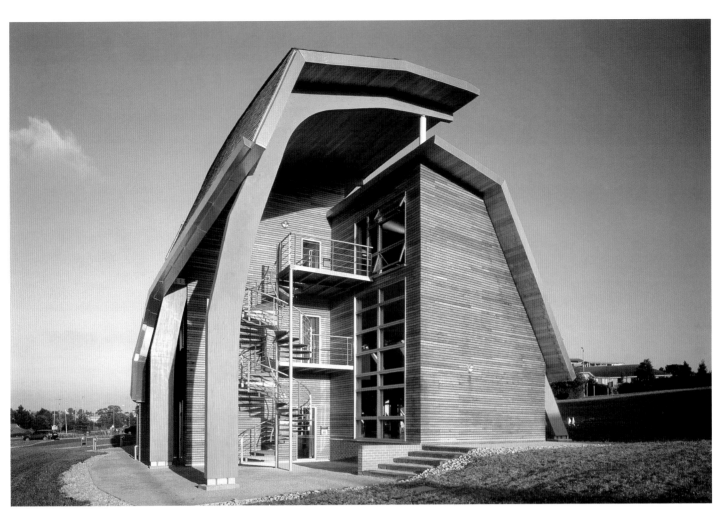

Window maker Velux required the building to have plenty of roof surface to act as a showcase for its products. For its Kettering office, White Design gave the company a roof that almost touches the ground. Seen from the main road, the 'roof' building is a good advertisement for Velux – using 95 of its windows.

Site plan

0 10 20

Ground floor plan

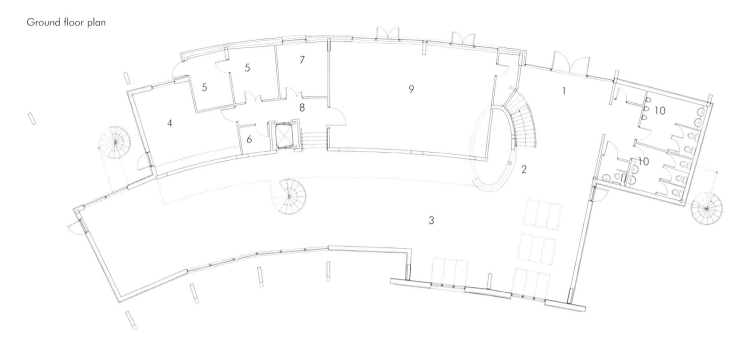

1. Entrance	6. Electrical plant / services	11. Void	16. Boardroom
2. Reception	7. Store	12. Open plan office	17. Services
3 .Display / exhibition	8. Lobby	13. Office	
4. Kitchen / staff room	9. Meeting room	14. Cloaks / store	
5. Plant room	10. Bathroom	15. Bridge	

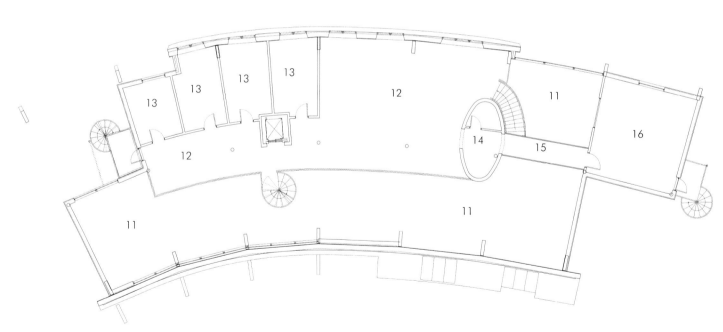

First floor plan

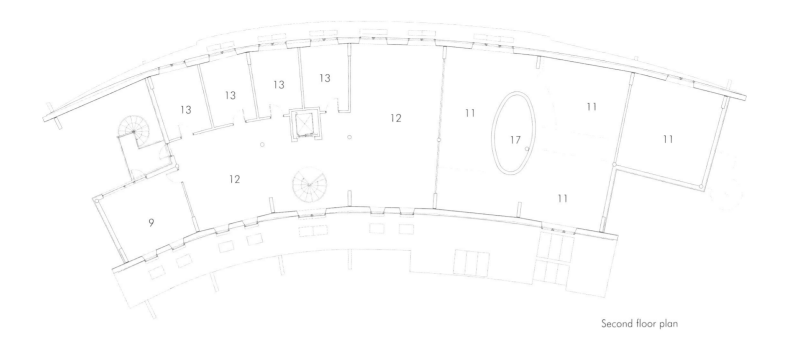

Second floor plan

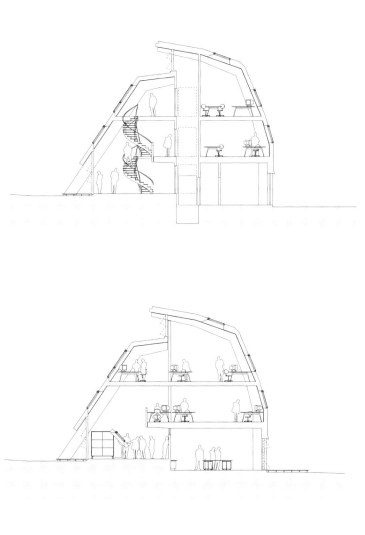

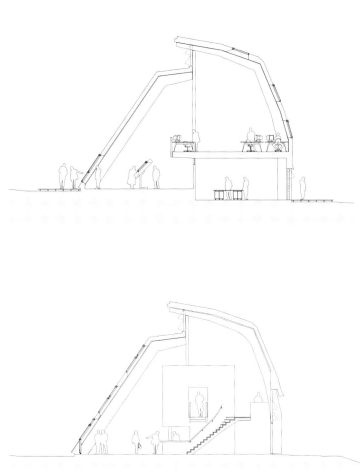

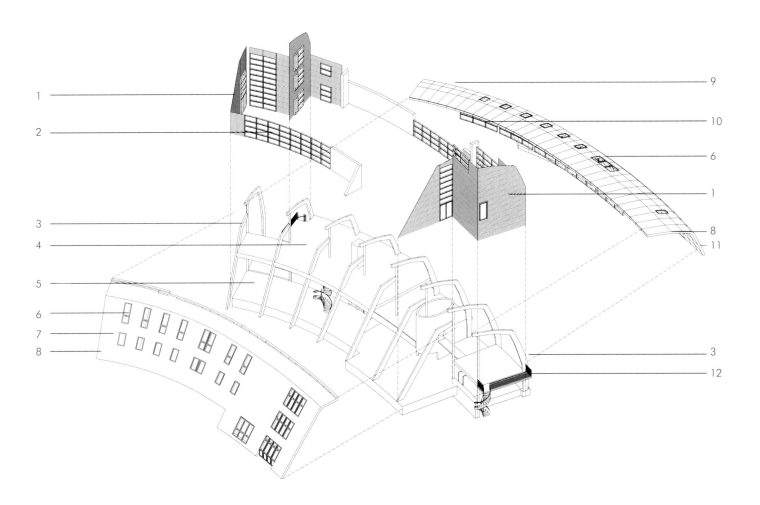

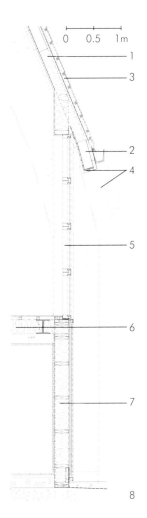

Detailed section through toilet and boardroom wall

1. 810x200 mm glulaminated "rib" frame

2. Glulaminated main purlins held off frame with galvanized brackets to form 75 mm gap between back "rib" roof finish

3. Roof made up of untreated cedar shingle (size varies with pitch) and counter battens; breather membrane/sarking 200-300 mm insulation; vapor check; and two layers of plasterboard

4. Pressed "natural finish" aluminum flashings (roof drops are shown dotted)

5. Windows linked to building management systems

6. Internal floor with main bearers and timber joists. Solid beech flooring, acoustic quilt over service void and suspended ceiling (to toilet areas only)

7. 250 mm stud infill with: 19x69 mm natural cedar boards on black painted counter battens; bitumen-impregnated fibreboard; 250 mm insulation; two layers of moisture-resistant plasterboard (toilet only); and tiling (toilet only)

8. In situ concrete slab with concrete infill and screed and tiling (toilet only). Office has raised flooring.

Axonometric view

1. Redwood cedar rainscreen

2. VELFAC window frames umber Grey RAL 7022

3. Timber Glulam

4. Suspended steel deck – finished in Junkers Beech flooring

5. In situ concrete floor – finished Junkers. Beech flooring

6. VELUX window frames umber grey RAL 7022

7. Natural state – Blue gray

8. Verges, Gutters & RWPs natural mill finish aluminum

9. Roof finish – redwood cedar shingles

10. Anodized VELFAC window frames

11. Underside of roof – Redwood cedar T&G boarding

12. Galvanized steel balcony handrails, treated softwood decking

ZEILON & PARTNERS

Lowe Brindfors Advertising

PHOTOGRAPHS: ÅKE E:SON LINDMAN

Stockholm, Sweden

The objective of this conversion was to create a functional working environment for the hundred employees of an advertising agency. The space available was an old coach house from the beginning of the century of considerable cultural value. Precisely due to the historical importance of the building, the local authorities stipulated that the conversion should not affect the original structure. Thus, the new building was conceived as a completely independent structural insert interwoven into the complex iron structure of the original space. With this strategy it was intended to differentiate the new elements from the old ones and thus respect the personality of the building.

A transparent space with industrial connotations is the nucleus of the new offices and evokes the spirit of the original space, a former building dating from the industrial revolution that has now been invaded by the flow of information and ideas of our era. This space has been divided both lengthwise and vertically into three areas distributed from the most private to the most public in both character and function. Thanks to the organization of the floor in different terraced levels and the distribution of the work areas, the employees can enjoy the views of the surroundings. This distribution also facilitates visual contact between the members of the agency and the differentiation of spaces according to the different work groups. Storage spaces act as barriers between the different levels.

A glass volume houses individual offices for employees who require a certain degree of privacy but must at the same time maintain visual contact with their colleagues. The lower level communicates directly with the terraced studio-workshop. The upper level is accessed by a ramp that is at the end of the meeting room, and is connected to the lower level by a staircase. This floor houses, at the rear of the entrance hall, the common areas such as the kitchen and the library, which act as transition spaces between the public and private areas. The meeting room is a natural continuation of the last terraced floor that stretches around the glass volume, thus unifying the different spaces. The individual offices are accessed by the long ramp. The sequence is completed with the management office and its corresponding reception area, with a staircase that leads directly to the entrance hall and the lower reception. The materials unify the different spaces and serve as a backdrop to the complex original structure, thus reinforcing the contrast between the new and the old.

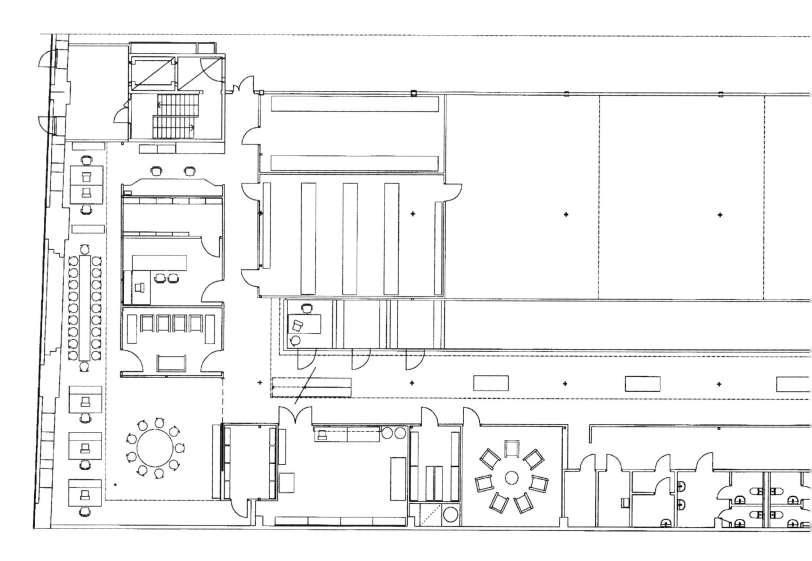

Ground floor plan

Longitudinal section

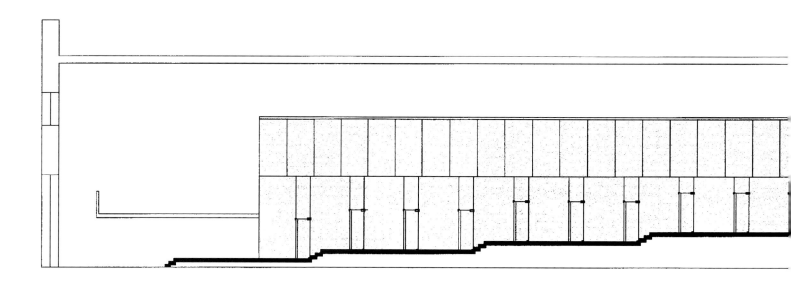

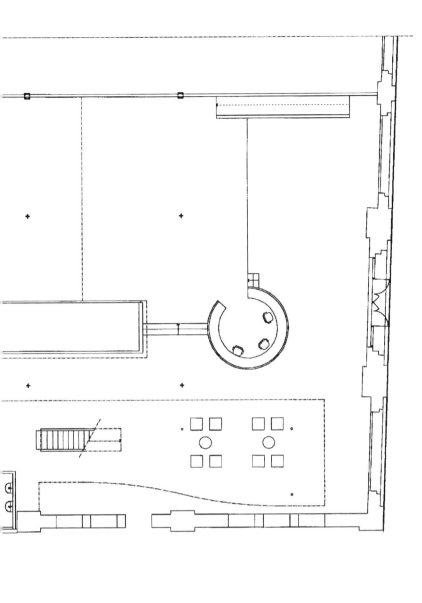

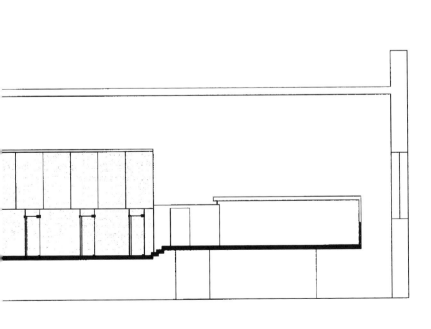

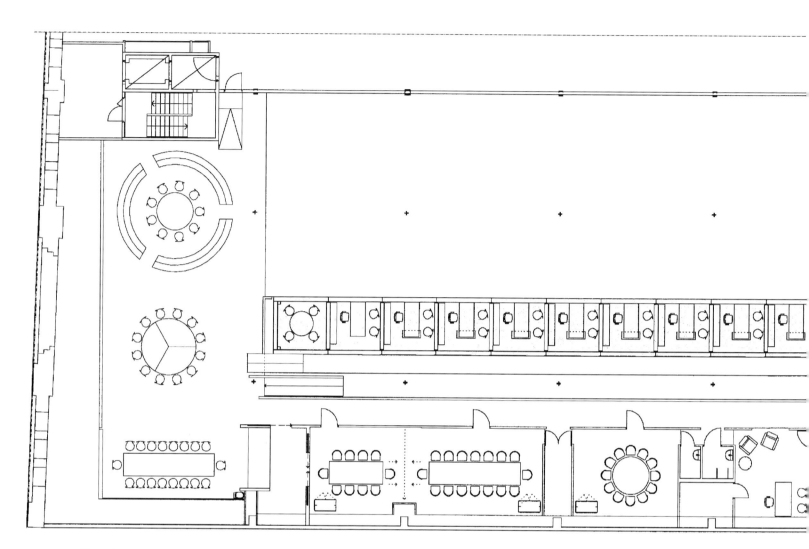

Mezzanine floor plan

Cross-section

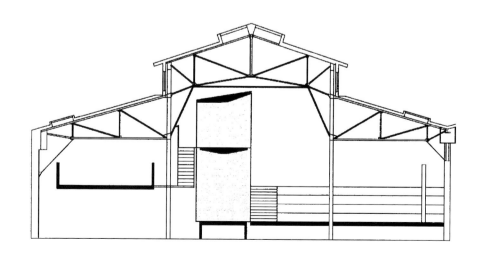

All technical supplies including ventilation, electricity, computer and telephone networking are supplied from underneath the ground floor level. This enabled the architects to preserve the original ceiling construction and its open character.

Large mast-like structures stepping uniform ly with the terrace levels in this open space provide indirect lighting which illuminate the original structure above.

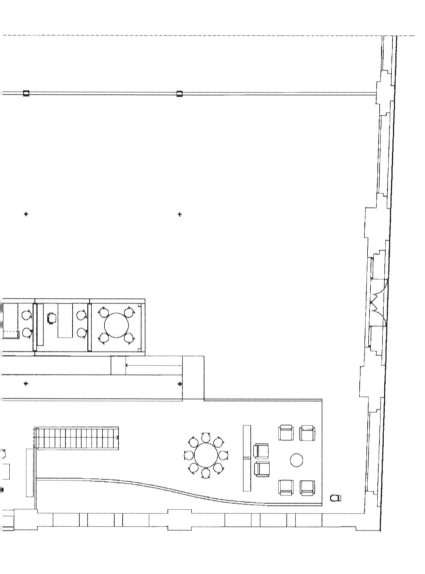

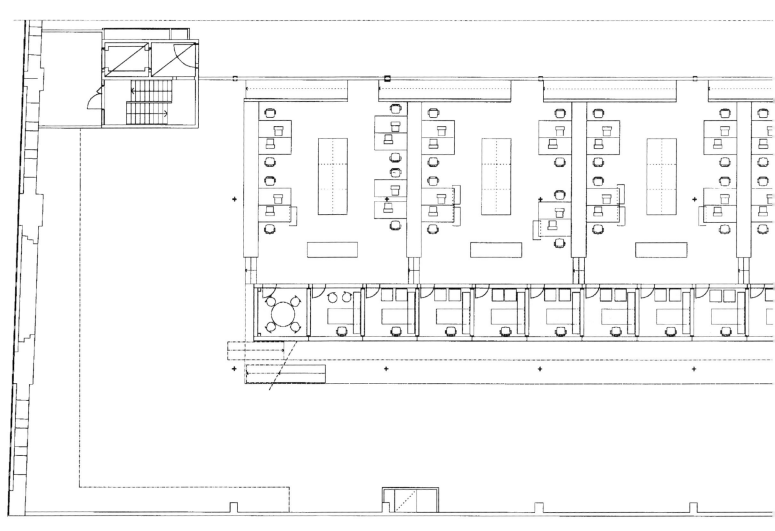

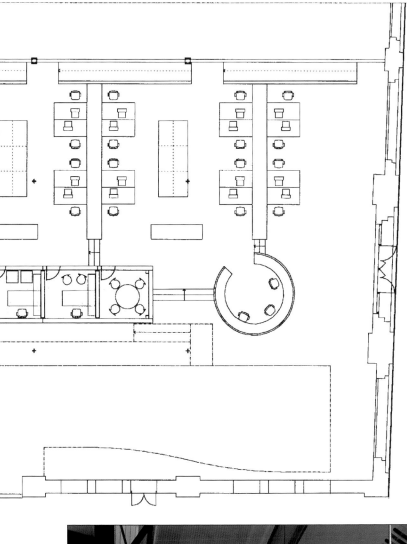

Production floor plan

Helfand Myerberg Guggenheimer

Architects' Office

Photographs: Paul Warchol

New York, USA

Representing the first collaboration of a new design partnership, the renovated 6,000 square feet, 13 foot-high industrial loft space, located in Soho, embodies the design principles of the firm: functional architecture rooted in the traditions of modernism that exploits simple geometry and ordinary materials to poetic effect. The programme called for 30 workstations, with extensive technical and material libraries, production areas and meeting spaces of various sizes. The result is an office design which synthesizes a lively, humane working environment while providing many different kinds of experiences, from private endeavour to group collaboration.

Slotted cleanly into the tall industrial space, new elements are simply and crisply expressed. Ordinary materials are used or finished in unexpected ways, animating and enlivening the straightforward layout. The free standing wall set parallel with the line of existing Corinthian columns demarcates the entrance and support spaces from the more general working areas and provides a remarkably effective sound sink, creating a tranquil and quiet working environment. Workstations and partitions are created from panellised oriented strand board (OSB), finished with aluminum dust.

Recycled ground rubber sheeting is used to clad the production screen walls, providing additional sound absorption and tack space. Existing strip flooring is given a luminous finish with bronze dust embedded in polyurethane.

Individual workstations are clustered together in four person pods, strung along a row of north-facing windows. The space between the workstations and dividing wall becomes a processional gallery for models and project material, leading to a large conference room at the elbow between the two wings. Partners' offices are organized behind a corrugated screen of shimmering translucent plastic panels that runs perpendicular to the main dividing wall.

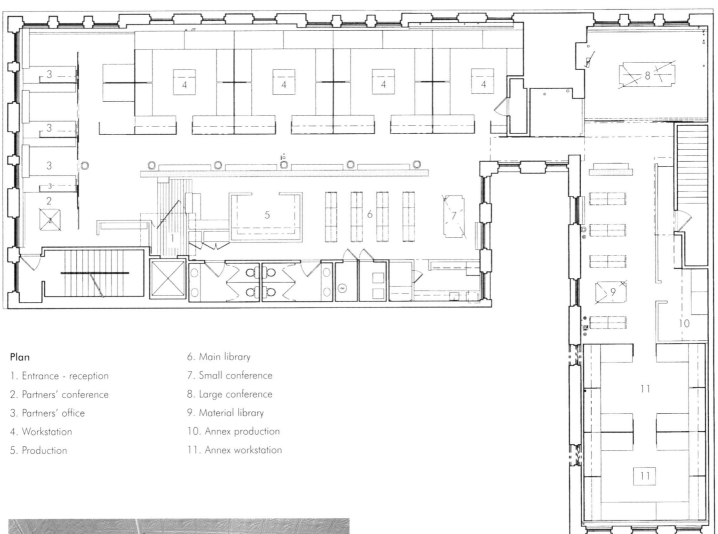

Plan

1. Entrance - reception
2. Partners' conference
3. Partners' office
4. Workstation
5. Production
6. Main library
7. Small conference
8. Large conference
9. Material library
10. Annex production
11. Annex workstation

A composite panel conceals the work area from visitors and defines a circulation space that leads to the secondary wing by way of the workshop, the main library and the small meeting room.

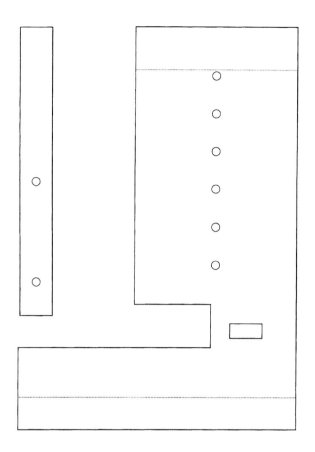

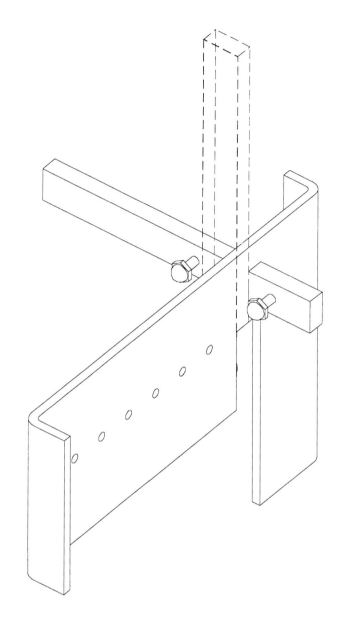

Details of the door pull

A series of four bent steel plate conference tables spanning from a single square to 1 1/2, 2 and 2 1/2 times the length, explore the geometry of intersecting plates required to support the four different rectangular tops.
The pull for the pivoting glass panel at the entry, a folded bronze scale model of the office floor plan, furnishes direct contact for each visitor with the conceptual design.

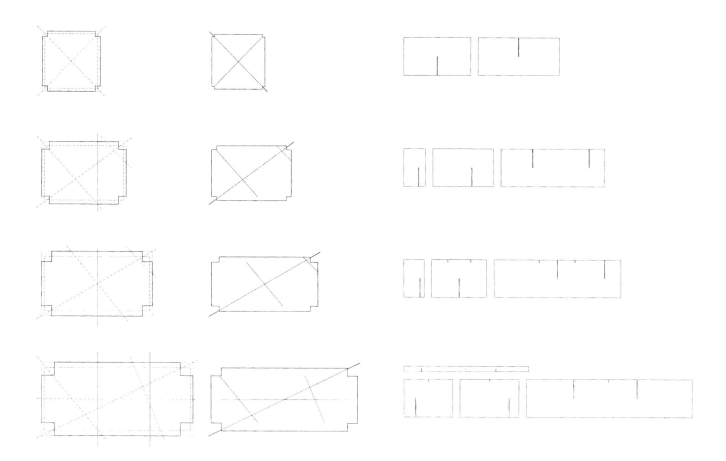

Detail of bent steel tables

The scheme expressed a prevailing desire to integrate all the spaces without losing the necessary independence of the work area. One of the solutions consists in using lightweight elements to separate the areas. Panels of translucent corrugated plastic separate the offices of the partners and allow natural light to filter into to the rest of the studio.

RAMÓN LLOPART RICART

Radio Barcelona

PHOTOGRAPHS: JOAN MUNDÓ

Barcelona, Spain

In architectural terms, the rehabilitation of Radio Barcelona goes beyond the building's physical alterations to become a prototype of regeneration in its field. This is demonstrated by the versatility of the different environments, multi-functionality of space, volumetric spaciousness that avoids closed compartments, the democratic and homogenized treatment of finishings, etc. This new concept consists of projecting a control center surrounded by the main studios. An idea of space hitherto unknown in the world of radio. So, by means of a closed-circuit television, there is communication with the other studios in the radio station. These are:

- Toresky Studio: a multi-functional studio for radio and television with all the possibilities of a great container for events, recording and audience.

- Caspe Studio: a studio that is visible from the street and is conceived as a multi-purpose studio -a 'radio boutique'- capable of broadcasting any of the programs or producing particular promotions. It is Radio Barcelona's showcase.

- News Studio: located on the first floor, with a direct view from the news section and connected by closed-circuit television to the control center, so that news may be broadcasted without the need to go down to the studio area.

Finally, and taking the ground floor at street level as a reference, this historic and emblematic point of union with the city opens some areas to the public, such as the vestibule, the Toresky Studio and the Caspe Studio.

The greatest techological potential, both in building technique and multimedia installations, is concentrated on the roof and in the basement. In the intermediate areas, above the offices and below the ground floor studios, we find workspaces where everything has been thought of to offer maximum comfort in a working environment.

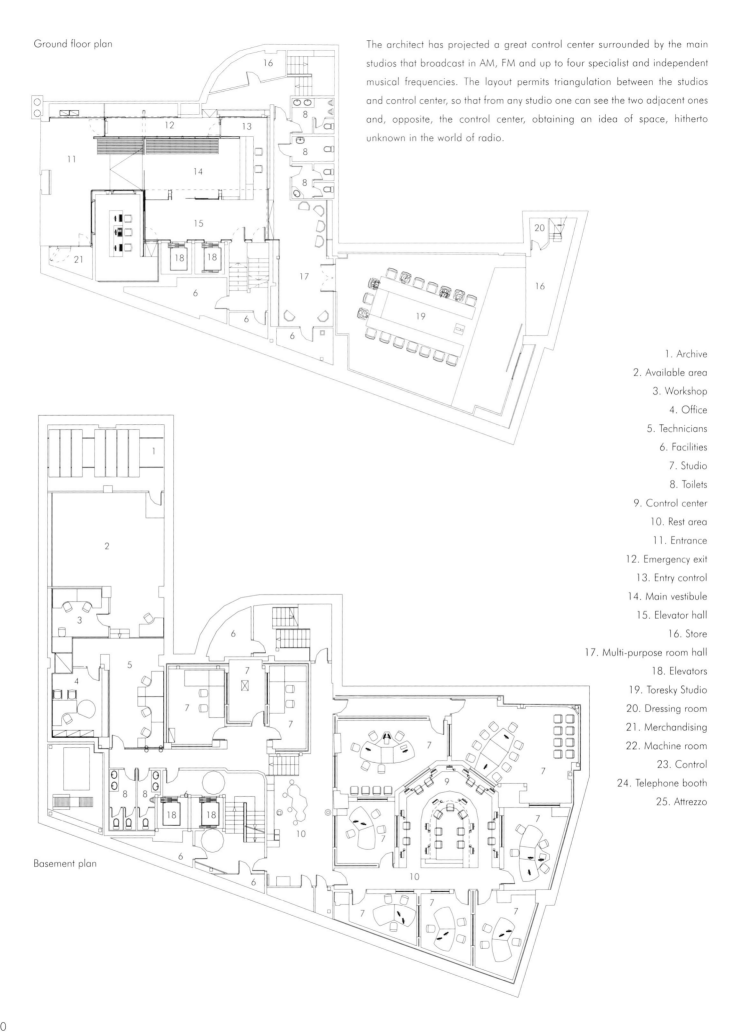

Ground floor plan

The architect has projected a great control center surrounded by the main studios that broadcast in AM, FM and up to four specialist and independent musical frequencies. The layout permits triangulation between the studios and control center, so that from any studio one can see the two adjacent ones and, opposite, the control center, obtaining an idea of space, hitherto unknown in the world of radio.

1. Archive
2. Available area
3. Workshop
4. Office
5. Technicians
6. Facilities
7. Studio
8. Toilets
9. Control center
10. Rest area
11. Entrance
12. Emergency exit
13. Entry control
14. Main vestibule
15. Elevator hall
16. Store
17. Multi-purpose room hall
18. Elevators
19. Toresky Studio
20. Dressing room
21. Merchandising
22. Machine room
23. Control
24. Telephone booth
25. Attrezzo

Basement plan

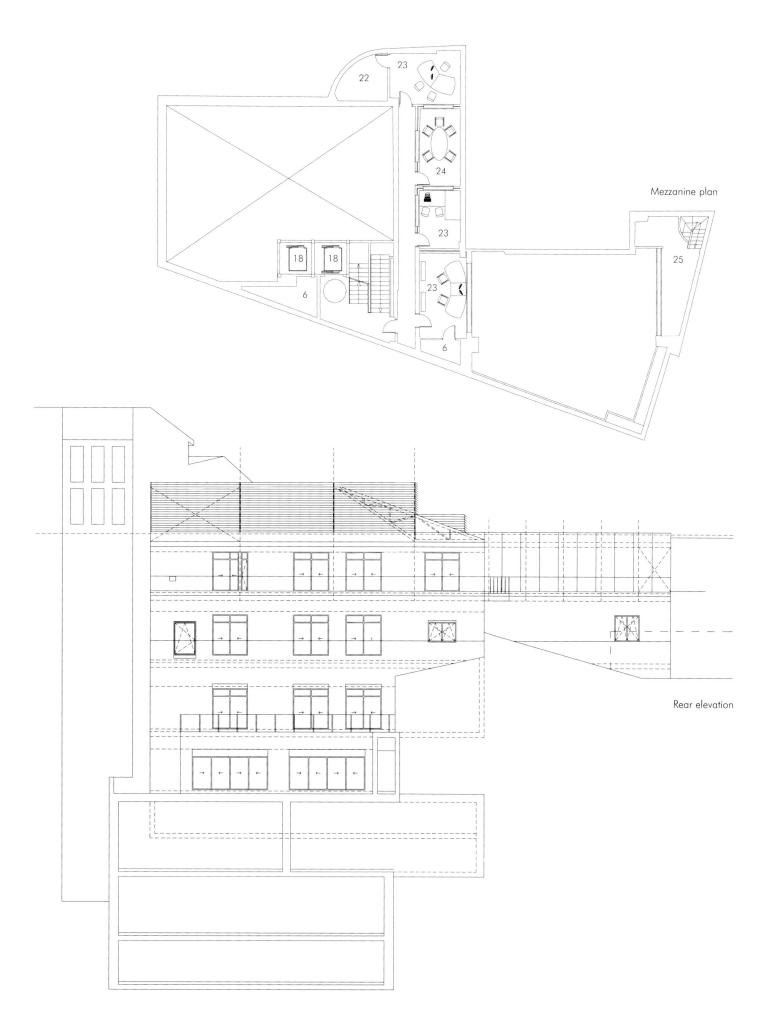

Mezzanine plan

Rear elevation

171

In the intermediate areas of the building, we find workspaces where everything has been thought of to offer maximum comfort in a working environment. This is demonstrated by the space segmentation with a view of other areas; also in the areas set side for relaxation, such as the terraces.

First floor plan

6. Facilities
8. Toilets
12. Emergency exit
18. Elevators
26. Office
27. Program management
28. Program area
29. Training classrooms
30. Meeting room
31. Creative area
32. Booth
33. News Studio
34. Radio formulas
35. Marketing
36. Reception
37. News management
38. Contents management

39. News area
40. Advanced areas
41. Terrace
42. Marketing management
43. Commercial area
44. Administration and sales
45. Sales area
46. Administration
47. General management
48. Boardroom
49. Meeting room
50. Cadena Ser management
51. General management secretary
52. Radio Barcelona management

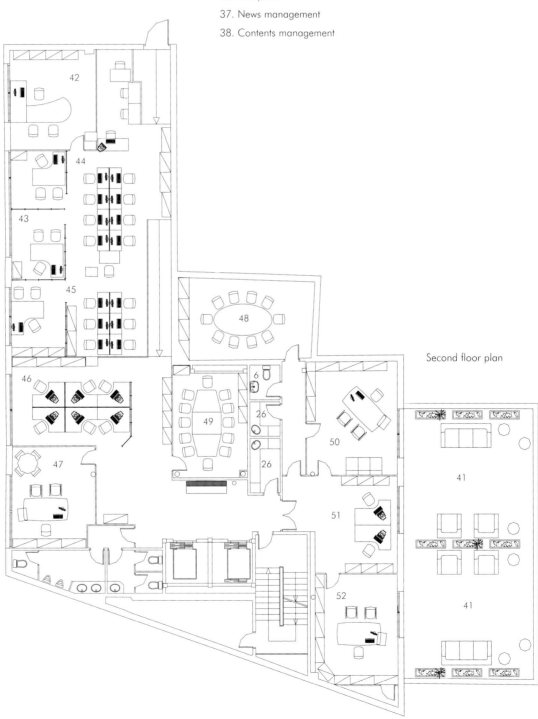

Second floor plan

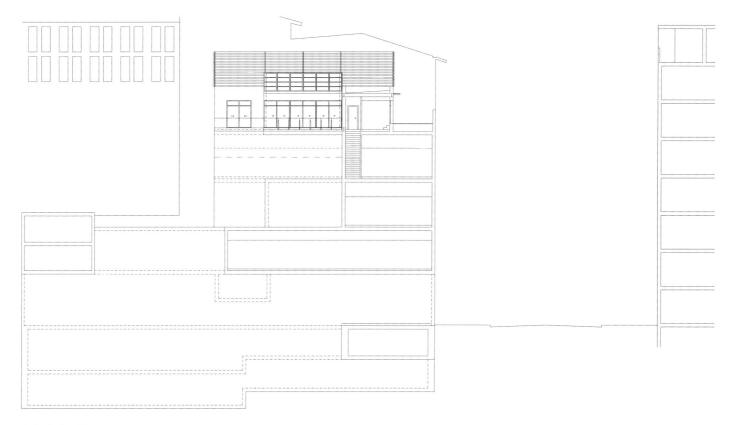

Lateral elevation

Front elevation

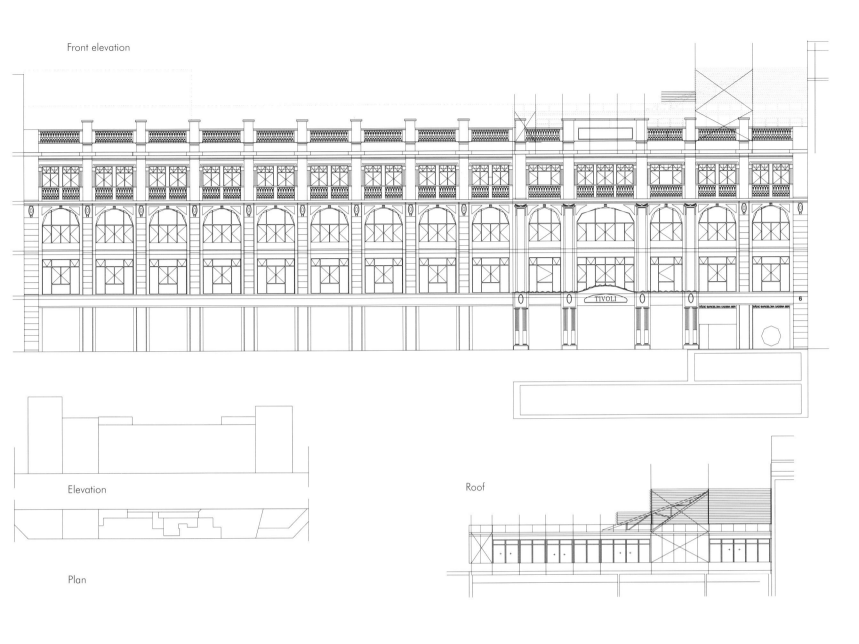

Elevation

Plan

Roof